بِسْمِ اللَّهِ الرَّحْمَنِ الرَّحِيمِ

Presented to ....

....

From ....

Date ....

Also by Harun Yahya

The Miracle in the Cell
The Miracle in the Eye
The Miracle in the Spider
The Miracle in the Gnat
The Miracle in the Ant
The Miracle in the Immune System
The Miracle of Creation in Plants
Ever Thought About the Truth
Devoted to Allah
Knowledge of the Qur'an
Qur'an Index
Migrating for the Cause of Allah
Epithets of Allah
Basic Concepts in the Qur'an
Answers from the Qur'an
The Moral Values of the Quran
Death, Resurrection, Hell
The Struggle of the Messengers
Religion of the Ignorant
The Arrogance of Satan
Prayer in the Qur'an
Conscience in the Qur'an
Day of Resurrection
Do Not Ever Forget
For Men of Understanding
Allah is Known by Wisdom
Allah is Known Through Reason
The Truth of the Life of the World
Eternity Has Already Begun
Timelessness and the Reality of Fate
Crude Understanding of Disbelief
Quick Grasp of Faith.

(All the above books are presently available in Turkish)

EVER THOUGHT ABOUT THE TRUTH?

*Does man not see that it is We Who created him
from sperm? Yet, behold! He stands forth as an
open adversary! And he makes comparisons for Us,
and forgets his own origin and Creation. He says,
"Who can give life to dry bones and decomposed
ones (at that)? Say, "He will give them life Who
created them for the first time! For He is Well-
versed in every kind of creation."*

(YA-SEEN, 77-79)

HARUN YAHYA

Goodword
B · O · O · K · S

First published in 2000
© Goodword Books 2002
Reprinted 2001, 2002 (twice)

GOODWORD BOOKS
1, Nizamuddin West Market
New Delhi 110 013
Tel. 435 5454, 435 1128, 435 6666
Fax 435 7333, 435 7980
e-mail: info@goodwordbooks.com

CONTENTS

ॐ

For "a community that can receive admonition"
and "men of understanding."

PART ONE

A NEW WORLD

ও

This is the way of Your Lord, leading straight: We have made plain Our revelations for those who receive admonition. (Al-Anaam, 126)

Those who listen to the Word, and follow the best (meaning) in it: those are the ones whom Allah has guided, and those are the ones endowed with understanding. (Az-Zumar, 18)

The principal aim of this book is to induce the reader to make a re-evaluation of matters which he may hither to have deemed quite insignificant, but which are actually the most important issues in his life. In the process, he shall have to keep his prejudices in abeyance until he has made a re-appraisal of those standards which till now, he has accepted as absolute.

We must bear in mind that when one approaches any given situation with prejudices, one is no longer able to make a healthy decision or reach a right conclusion about it. As a matter of fact, when one wants to see something as right, one sees it as right. One perceives a thing as evil since one has already decided beforehand that it is so.

The telling point about these prejudices and presuppositions that they are rarely formed by the individual himself. From the beginning of his life, he is burdened with the countless prejudices that society instills in him. Family, friends and close relations determine his value-judgements the media especially have a great capacity to condition people's attitudes toward certain subjects. Newspapers and television regularly misrepresent the right as unpleasant, unacceptable and even harmful, while showing the wrong to be good and desirable.

One who readily accepts these prejudices instilled by society, loses a great part of his personality. He acts under the influence of conditioning by others, and does not behave with a free will or mind. Others' predispositions determine his behaviour. He can thus accept only the values that are shown to be true as true. Moreover, when we consider that different societies with different cultural backgrounds happen to believe in different rights and wrongs, we can see that there is not much sense in following the dictates of any given society without questioning its value-judgements. By the same token, what is currently agreed to be wrong and immoral may well be considered acceptable in the future. Eating human flesh is very normal for cannibals, and obeying a crazy leader in a fascist society like Nazi Germany was absolutely right for the people who followed and supported him at that time. The number of examples is legion. What we must stress is that cogitating independently upon society's conditioning, is conduct which betokens wisdom in the thinker. Such a person is necessarily aware that the "values" imposed by society may be wrong and may lead to ethical dilemmas if adopted.

Religion - especially today- is one of the most important subjects about which countless prejudices are produced by society. The influence at least of some part of the media has formed many prejudices about religion, which are hard to overcome.

As a result of these prejudices in our societies, religion has become a concept which most people either do not consider important, or believe they do not need to think about, preferring to stay away from it as far as possible. People who fit this definition cannot be said, however, to have adopted such an attitude consciously. For them, religion is an irrelevant subject that is of no benefit to them. On the contrary, it places some restrictions upon them. One having such a point of view would claim, when asked, that he is a Muslim, although religion may be one of the less important matters of his life and one of the subjects of which he is quite ignorant.

Indeed, such a person would never have given any serious thought to religion, not even for once in his life. He would probably never have thought seriously about questions like "What is the purpose of life, why do I exist? Why does the concept of 'religion' exist?" etc. For him, religion is a matter that generally concerns aged people, that presents some ethical values, but mostly entails many boring, tedious prohibitions and restrictions. He practices some of the religious rituals on religious holidays, and festivals and on some important days like the death of a relative, but he finds only a few of these formal rituals right and necessary and consider certain others as ancient and "outdated". Although he usually does not deny religion, he tries, as we have mentioned before, to keep away from it as far as possible.

This wrong perception of religion originates from accepting presuppositions imposed by some part of society without subjecting them to independent scrutiny. However, reasoning and pondering on every aspect of life are very important issues for human beings, the power of reason being what makes them different from animals. In the Qur'an, the ultimate ethical guidebook, the importance of thinking is emphasized in many verses as follows:

"Say: 'To whom belong the earth and all beings therein? Say, if you know!' They will say, 'To Allah!' Say: 'Yet will you not receive admonition?'" (Al-Mumenoon, 84-85)

"And We have indeed made the Qur'an easy to understand and remember: then is there any that will receive admonition?" (Al-Qumar, 17)

"...This is Allah your Lord; therefore serve Him you: will you not receive admonition" (Yunus, 3)

"Is He then Who creates like one who cannot create ? Will you not receive admonition?" (An-Nahl, 17)

Those who cannot think about religion independently of society's conditioning will make two great mistakes. The first of these is not being aware of the real purpose of religion, and therefore as a result of trying to avoid religion - not being aware of Allah.

The second fault is supposing that religion exists to drag people to an awkward and bigoted position full of pressures, and to impose duties on people, which go against their very nature. One of the principal reasons for the "religion is boring" syndrome is the insistent manner of a group of people-supposedly acting in the name of Allah—who display and promote the aforementioned negativity, although such an approach has no bearing whatsoever upon true religion.

Once the individual rectifies the first mistake and starts becoming acquainted with the Creator and the Creator's attributes, he also rids himself of the superstitions that keep him away from religion. The correction of the first fault brings him a sharpness of mind and a sensitivity which in turn help him to correct the second fault as well. They give him the ability to separate true religion from false structures disguised as religion. Then the individual will realize that religion is easy to live by and brings real happiness, well being and freedom to his life.

In short, the society we live in has formed countless

prejudices about religion. However, in approaching religion, the basic criterion must be its original references, like the Qur'an, and not peoples' sayings about religion. In the Qur'an, it has been indicated that following the "common run of the people" does not necessarily lead us to Allah's way.

> *"If you were to follow the common run of those on this earth, they would lead you away from the way of Allah. They follow nothing but conjecture: they do nothing but lie." (Al-Anaam, 116)*

When a person stops "following the herd" and begins to think with his soul, he personally sees the reality emphasized in the Qur'anic verse cited above. He steps into a new world which is quite different from that of the "common run of the people". This step will drive away from him the darkness, distress, and troubles of his old life and bring to him the countless graces and the deep wisdom of religion.

Before you read through the rest of the book, let us remind you that the word "religion" refers to Islam alone, as "The only true faith in Allah's sight is Islam." (Al Imran, 19)

BASIC QUESTIONS

ᕽ

Were they created of nothing, or were they themselves the creators?

Or did they create the heavens and the earth? Surely, they have no firm belief.

Or are the treasures of your Lord with them, or have they control over them? (At-Tur,, 35-37)

As mentioned before, the first error a prejudiced person makes is trying to evaluate religion without giving thought to Allah. Sociologists, for example, who do research on religion, can write thousands of books on how religions arose and how they affected societies sociologically. Yet, in spite of all these great academic studies, they cannot understand religion even to a minute extent when compared with those who lead their lives within the boundaries of religion.

Such people are not capable of comprehending the reality of Allah's unity, which is the basis of religion. Anyone who decides to learn about Islam needs first to understand the existence of Allah. If he does not believe in Allah, he will simply be investigating the Qur'an and Muslims in terms of his own limited vision of life.

The Qur'an thus expresses disapproval of such people: "They disbelieve what they cannot grasp, for they have not yet seen its prophecy fulfilled." (Yunus, 39) Islam is not a man-made ideology about which half-baked ideas and baseless conclusions can be put forth from the outside. The individual can understand what Islam is about only when he understands the existence of Allah and lives his life as enjoined in the Qur'an.

Essentially, the existence of Allah and the reality that there is no deity other than Allah are crystal clear facts. But in "the society of ignorance" where people fail to use their reasoning due to their habit of indifference and indolence, they grow blind and cannot comprehend this reality. As a matter of fact, that is the reason why they were stigmatized as a "society of ignorance" (Jahilliyah).

One of the many Qur'anic verses about pondering on the existence of Allah records the Almighty's advice to the Prophet on how he should address the ignorant:

> "Say: 'Think, you, if Allah took away your hearing and your sight, and sealed up your hearts, who - a god other than Allah - could restore them to you?'" The same verse goes on to say: "See how We explain the signs by various symbols; yet they turn aside." (Al-Anaam, 46)

A brief example can help us enrich our views and remove our innate ignorance.

Let's assume that there is a person from whose memory everything, including the knowledge of his self-being and his body, has been wiped out. If he found himself on a place like earth, what would he feel like? He would undoubtedly be so amazed and so astonished as to lose his mind out of curiosity. The first thing he would notice would probably be his body. He would not be aware that his body in fact belonged to him in the first place, thinking of it as an external object, like the other things in the scene. Then it would be very interesting for him to be able to control his body parts and make them do what he wanted them to do. He would probably try to figure out the use of his arm by moving it up and down for a while.

He would find very suitable surroundings for his body, the reason for the existence of which would still be unknown to him. There would be safe ground to stand on, a clear image to view, beautiful fragrances to smell, various animals, a proper air temperature exactly suitable to the body, an atmosphere suitable for breathing, and thousands of other sensitive balances. Edible fruits to satisfy his hunger, pure and clear water to cool his parched throat and many more things.

For a moment, let us put ourselves in his position and reflect for a while. In a place like this, would we just go and enjoy ourselves, or be wise enough to ask ourselves some very crucial questions? Would we try to understand who we were, why we were there, what the reason for our existence was, what the reason for the existence of the present order was or, would we simply ignore these questions and be concerned with how much we enjoyed our lives? Would not the first questions come to our minds be as follows:

Who am I?

Who has created me, who has created this perfect body of mine?

Who has created this great order which surrounds me?

What does He, who created everything, want from me? What does He want to show me?

Even an individual with a weak mind would think that there is nothing more important than finding answers to these questions. Someone who pays no attention to them, preferring rather to spend his life in fulfilling his physical needs, amusing himself during the day and sleeping at nights, would undoubtedly be a creature of no understanding at all. Someone must have created his body and his surroundings, and they must have come into being all of a sudden. Once he was created, every second of the rest of his life must also have been dependent on that Superior Being, who had initially created him. What could be more important than knowing about this Superior Being, who obviously possesses a great power?

Let us continue with our example and assume that he reaches a city after walking through the land for a while. There are various types of people there, most of whom are pretty vulgar, ambitious and insincere. And almost nobody is thinking about his Owner or the place he is living in. Although everyone has a job, an aim or an ideology, the people of the city cannot bring good order to the city, with which everyone would be content.

Let's assume he meets some people whom the denizens of the city dislike, and towards whom they feel rage and enmity. As to what these people are like, he sees that they are significantly different from the others in many ways. He feels that, as human beings, they are amiable reasonable, and trustworthy. They look humble and they speak in a clear, moderate and sensible manner. He can easily see that there is nothing wrong with them, so he becomes confused and has doubts as to why the citizenry think otherwise.

Let's assume he starts a conversation with them and they tell him: "We have a different view of life and think differently from other people because we are aware that there is an Owner of this place and everything in it. We are also aware that His power is above everything and He has created this place and everything else to test and educate us until the day comes when we will leave this place. We have a book which we have received from Him, and we are leading our lives in accordance with this book."

In such a situation, he might not be a hundred per cent sure whether these people were really telling the truth or not. But he would probably understand that what they were talking about was quite important. He would feel there was nothing more important than obtaining further information about these people at that moment, and he would be extremely curious about the book they were talking about, would he not?

The only thing that stops us from being as sensible as the person in this example is our having been on this earth for a longer period of time. We have experienced a growth process instead of coming into being as an adult all of a sudden, like the person in the story. Consequently, we have to admit that most of us are in a position similar to that of the town people in the example due to our disregard of such questions in our lives. What we should further bear in mind is that almost none of the people in this city actually thought about the questions cited above, found some consistent answers on their own, and finally turned away from the Superior Being, Who created them. In fact, most of them did not even go through these steps, but simply pushed these questions aside and stopped thinking about them, because of their "collective ignorance".

Are we aware of the fact that the "society of ignorance" we are living in prevents us from answering those crucial questions mentioned above by keeping us occupied with questions like: "What shall I eat tonight, which dress should I wear tomorrow?" or "What is she thinking about me, what should I say to him?"? Unfortunately, this shows nothing but abysmal ignorance although we claim to be living in the "information age".

Now, you have a chance! Think about the complete ignorance you might have been exposed to by such a "society of ignorance" and ask yourselves the following question, which so far you might not have thought over, or might have brushed aside with insufficient explanations: How did I come into existence?

In order to be able to answer this question, it would be useful to start with the physical beginning of our existence and think about that extraordinary event - "birth".

The brief history of birth can be summarized as follows:

Sperms are produced literally 'outside' of a man's body. The reason for this is the fact that sperm production can occur only in a suitable environment with a temperature of about 35 degrees Celsius, which is two degrees below the average body temperature. Male testicles are the only body parts with this temperature, as they are rightly placed outside of the body. To bring the temperature to the required level, another mechanism is activated. The skin covering the testicles shrinks when it is cold and sweats when it is hot to keep the temperature of this area stable. Approximately a thousand sperms are produced per minute, and they have a special design that eases their long journey from the man's testicles to the woman's egg. A sperm comprises a head, a neck and a tail by the use of which a fish-like movement towards the mother's uterus takes place.

The head part, which carries the genetic code of the future human being, is covered with a special protective armour. The benefit of this armour is noticed at the entrance of the mother's uterus. This place is very acidic to protect the mother from microbes and other alien particles like sperms, but by the use of this armour, most sperms manage to stay alive.

Not only sperms are ejaculated to the uterus. Semen is a mixture that consists of many other liquids. These liquids contain sugar that supplies energy to the sperms. Semen, which is a base in its chemical form, neutralizes the acidic environment at the entrance of the uterus and creates a safe environment for sperms. It also makes the environment slippery so that sperms can move along easily. Sperms make a difficult journey inside the body of the mother until they reach the egg. No matter how hard they try to survive, only a thousand sperms out of 200-300 million can make it to the egg.

In the light of this brief information, let's try to find the answers to some questions that cross our minds: How can a sperm make itself so suitable for entry into the mother's uterus, about which it knows nothing beforehand? How can a sperm be produced in the male body in a way that it can survive and find its way to the egg in the female uterus in spite of the protective mechanisms of the female body, about which the sperm had no previous idea? How can this happen?

Since a sperm lacks the ability to adapt itself to an unknown environment in advance, the only possible answer to these questions is that it is actually created that way.

Let's continue with the brief story of birth:

An egg is about half the size of a salt grain. The place where an egg and a sperm meet is called the Fallopian tube. The egg secretes a special fluid that leads the sperms to the egg. As they come closer to the egg, their protective armour is melted by another fluid secreted by the egg. As a result, solvent enzyme sachets appear on the cover of the sperms' heads. By the use of these enzymes, the sperm that is to fertilize the egg, penetrates the membrane of the egg. When the sperms surround the egg, they race one another to enter to the egg. Mostly, only one sperm fertilizes the egg and from that time on, there is no possibility for another sperm to enter it. Before fertilization, the electric charge of the sperms and the egg are opposite, therefore they attract each other. However, after the entrance of the first sperm, the electrical charge of the egg changes, acquiring a pushing effect on the rest of the sperms.

Finally, the DNA of the male present in the sperm combines with the DNA of the female. At this moment, there forms a new cell (the zygote), that is, a new human being inside the mother's womb.

After considering this bit of information, a new question comes to our minds: How is it that an egg is prepared to welcome a sperm as if it "knew" that it would meet the sperm? How can this happen? The only possible answer to this question is that the egg is created to be suitable to the sperm by the will of a Creator who has also created the sperms and controls both the sperm and the egg.

The extraordinary nature of birth does not finish with all this. The fertilized egg clings on to the womb by its special knobbly surface. The small protuberances on the surface of the egg jut out and penetrate deep into the mother's womb like the roots of plants in the ground. The zygote starts to develop through hormones secreted by the mother. The egg keeps receiving nutrition provided by the mother.

With time, the cells divide and grow in number by the two-four-eight-sixteen model. In the beginning, all cells that are formed by the division of old ones have the same properties as each other. Then, all of a sudden, newly formed cells somehow start differentiating, showing separate characteristics, as they are to form different organs of the fetus. The science of today still lacks the competence to give a satisfactory answer to the question of why and how exactly this differentiation of cells takes place and how they form different organs with such perfect organization.

As time passes, a drastic change takes place in the jelly-like fetus. Relatively rough bones start to form inside that soft structure, all of them surprisingly, in their proper places. What's amazing here, is that while all the cells carry exactly the same characteristics at the beginning, through the differentiating process, some of them turn out to be eye cells sensitive to light, others become nerve cells that perceive heat while yet others form those cells that detect sound vibrations.

Finally the fetus' construction is completed and a new baby is born into the world. At this stage, it is 100 million times bigger and 6 billion times heavier than its initial form when it was a fertilized egg.

This "brief history" mentioned above concerns us, because it is the story of how we came into being. For us, what can be more important than finding the ultimate Cause and Owner of that great, extraordinary and complex event of our existence? When we glance at this short history, we come across many other questions to which science, which is under the influence of materialism, has not yet found any answers.

But there are still many questions that need to be answered. One of these is: How can cells of the same structure start to gather in groups and form different organs of the body while they multiply?

Actually, there is no answer to these questions about birth other than accepting the presence of a Creator. It would be a great mistake to think that all of these complex operations occur on their own or by chance. How can cells agree to form "human organs"? Let's think about this a little further. Let's assume that there are two wise adults who come together and decide to work on an engineering project. Even between these two persons, some misunderstandings will unavoidably occur and this will put the success of the project at risk. Then, how can thousands and millions of cells work together to form an absolutely perfect organization without any mishap? Who would dare to say an answer to this question: "It may be possible by chance"? Some atheist "scientists" of today explain this marvellous occurrence as the "magic of nature". What does this mean? Who or what is nature? Has not nature also been created?

Another attempt to answer this question might be to refer to the mother and the father—which would be meaningless. The role of parents in this event is in fact, neglible. Neither mother nor the father is aware what goes on within them in the production of gender cells, fertilization and development of fetus. The exact date of birth is unknown to mother who has no control over delivery. In spite of this, mother and father are seen as the "origin of one's life"? But are they so?

The mother and father are very important to their child, as they play a role in his existence. On the other hand, one never, or only rarely, thinks about ones real Creator. Is not the real Creator, who has the ultimate power and control ones everything including birth, life and death, worth more love and respect? His existence is clear and the existence of any other thing without Him is not possible. No one but Allah can create anyone or any matter on his own, while He neither begets nor is begotten as is stated in the third verse of Al-Ikhlas 3.

The creation is explained in the Qur'an as follows;

"We created man from a quintessence (of clay);

Then We placed him as (a drop of) sperm in a place of rest, firmly fixed;

Then We made the sperm into a clot of congealed blood; then of that clot We made a (fetus) lump; then We made out of that lump bones and clothed the bones with flesh; then We developed out of it another

creature. So blessed be Allah, the noblest of Creators!"
(Al-Mumenoon, 12-14)

This being so, it is clear that there is no difference between ourselves and that man in the story, who was "suddenly" created and become curious about who had created him and everything around him. Of course, he found himself as an adult and without any parents who gave birth to him and raised him. But now that we also know that our coming into existence can in no way be explained by parents, we can consider our situation similar to that of the man in the story.

In such a situation, the most important thing to do is to search exclusively for the truth, to listen to those who claim they have knowledge and evidence about the truth and then to think over what we have been told. Take the man in the story again. As we know, he meets some people in the city who tell him that they can make known to him the Creator Who has created him and everything around and that there is a book from Him. What do you think he would do? Would he listen to them, or would he simply turn away from them and prefer to be involved with such ordinary, everyday questions like: "What shall I wear tonight, what shall I say to him?" That are daily repeated and will one day become meaningless when death comes to him. Which one of these two choices is the more rational, logical and conscientious? You, without doubt, know the correct answer for this man. But, what about yourself?

What leads up to the event of creation is specifically described in certain other verses of the Qur'an;

"Does man think that he will be left uncontrolled, without purpose?

Was he not a drop of sperm emitted in lowly form?

Then he became a leech-like clot; then Allah made and fashioned him in due proportion.

And of him He made two sexes, male and female.

Has not He, the same, the power to give life to the dead?" (Al-Qiyama, 36-40)

"Allah created you from dust; then from a sperm-drop; then He made you in pairs. No female conceives, or lays down her load, but with His knowledge. No man is long-lived, nor is a part cut off from his life, but in accordance with His Decree. All this is easy to Allah." (Fatir, 11)

The human is a being created by Allah and as a created entity, he cannot change this fact. He cannot bring any other explanation to his own existence. Since he has been created, he would not be left uncontrolled and irresponsible as emphasized in the above verses. There is, of course, a purpose for creation. Where then will he find the answer?

There is only one answer to this question and that is in the book that Allah has sent down to him.

PONDERING ON
THE QUR'AN
∾

It is We Who have created you: why then will you not witness the Truth?

Do you then see?— The human seed that you discharge— Is it you who create it, or We?

We have decreed Death to be your common lot, and We are not to be frustrated...

...And you certainly know already the first form of creation: why then do ye not celebrate His praises?

Consider the seed that you sow in the ground. Is it you that cause it to grow, or are We the Cause? Were it Our Will, We could crumble it to dry powder, and you would be left in wonderment...

Consider the water which you drink. Do you bring it down as rain from the cloud, or do We? Were it Our Will, We could make it salt and unpalatable: then why do you not give thanks?

Observe the fire which you kindle. Is it you who grow the tree which feeds the fire, or do We grow it?...

...Then celebrate with praises the name of your Lord, the Supreme!

I swear by the shelter of the stars (a mighty oath if you but knew it) that this is indeed a Qur'an Most Honourable,

In Book well-guarded,

Which none shall touch but those who are clean:

A Revelation from the Lord of the Worlds.

Is it such a Message that you would hold it in light esteem? (Al-Waqia, 57-81)

What do you know about the Qur'an?

In most of the Middle Eastern countries where Muslims are in the majority, most of the people who can be considered as "average citizens" would give this answer: "The Qur'an is the holy book of our religion." Yet, they know very little about the content of the Qur'an, about what is written in its pages.

In fact, the Qur'an is used for many purposes which are far removed from its true revealed purpose. It is usually hung on the walls of houses within a decorative cover and read usually by elder people from time to time. People read it in Arabic, but as they only know how to read Arabic letters without understanding the meaning, most of the time they have no idea what they have been reading about, as so have no grasp of the content of the Qur'an.

The Qur'an is also supposed to afford some very interesting benefits to people. After reading it and performing some weird rituals like breathing hard on another person's face, the readers and his close relatives are believed to be protected from a possible future "accident or misfortune". The Qur'an is credited with being some sort of amulet that includes talismanic words which protect people against bad luck. The Qur'an is also believed to have a frightening power: it smites people if they tell lies! At graveyards it is read out for the deceased without anyone knowing what is being read. It can even be used for telling fortunes.

In short, in most of the countries where Muslims are in the majority, only a small percentage of people know the content of the Qur'an and ponder on the Qur'an as required. As a result, people who are ignorant of the real message of the Qur'an, attribute different meanings to it. Many people believe some traditions to have their origin in the Qur'an, although they may be contradictory to the very nature of the Qur'anic message. For example, there are many people who believe that a blue bead, which is believed to possess the power to avert the devil's eye, is recommended in the Qur'an.

Then what is the true nature of the Qur'an? The answer must be derived from the Qur'an itself, as that is where the truth is to be found.

> *"Here is a Message for mankind: Let them take warning from it, and let them know that He is no other than the One Allah: let men of understanding take heed." (Ibrahim 52)*

> *"And We have indeed made the Qur'an easy to understand and remember: but will any take heed?" (Al-Qamar, 32)*

> *"There is, in their stories, instruction for men endued with understanding. It is not a tale invented, but a confirmation of what went before it,- a detailed exposition of all things, and a guide and a mercy to any such as believe." (Yusuf, 111)*

> *"This is the Book; in it is certain and unmistakable guidance for those who fear Allah." (Baqara, 2)*

These verses and many others emphasize that the real purpose of the revelation of the Qur'an is to encourage people to ponder on such crucial issues as the creation and purpose of life, to make them know about Allah Who has created them, and to guide them to the right way. The Qur'an is a book that is needed by people with an open mind and soul.

Many rituals, believed to have originated from the Qur'an, are widely practiced, but in fact are not from the Qur'an. On the contrary, they conflict with the Qur'anic message. This shows us that there is a huge difference between the true religion as explained in the Qur'an and the concept of religion generally prevalent. This difference has been caused by abandoning the real source, the Qur'an. Of this the Qur'an says;

> "Then the Messenger will say: 'O my Lord! Truly my people took this Qur'an for just foolish nonsense.'" (Al-Furqan, 30)

Therefore, what is needed in the first place is to correct this wrong point of view about the Qur'an and make people understand that the Qur'an is not a book which is addressed only to the apostle but to all people who consider themselves Muslims. Any person who utters this well-known statement: "I'm a Muslim, alhamdulillah" must read the Qur'an and try to understand the meaning of the verses. In the Qur'an, the importance of learning verses and reciting them is especially emphasized.

> "And recite what is rehearsed to you in your homes, of the Signs of Allah and His wisdom: for Allah understands the finest mysteries and is well-acquainted with them" (Al-Ahzab, 33)

Because of not doing what is ordered in the Qur'an, and not learning the religion from its original source, countless prejudices which stem from traditions, have been introduced into religion. The verses of the Qur'an strongly emphasize that, in order to understand religion, there is no need to look for any source other than the Qur'an:

"Say: 'Shall I seek for any judge other than Allah? - when He it is Who has sent to you the Book, explained in detail.' They know full well, those to whom We have given the Book, that it hath been sent down from your Lord in truth. Never be then of those who doubt." (Al-Anaam, 114)

"What is the matter with you? How do you judge you? Will you not then receive admonition? Or have you a manifest authority? Then bring your Book of authority if you be truthful!" (As-Saaffat 154-157)

Of course, learning the Qur'an is only an introductory step, since application should follow it. Some people believe that the Qur'an addresses only Muslims of the 7th century, while others think that only a small number of the verses address people other than the Muslims of the 7th century. One of such a mentality is satisfied just with reading the Qur'an and thinks he has fulfilled his religious duties by so doing. However, it is not only a matter of learning what is in the Qur'an, but also putting it into practice, fulfilling the duties ordered in the Qur'an, adopting the moral standards explained in the Qur'an, in short applying the Qur'an to one's own everyday life.

Those who claim that the Qur'an has become outdated and needs to be revised to be in accordance with this new age, cannot grasp the fact that the Qur'an is not confined by chains of time, but covers all ages and societies, as it has been revealed by Allah, Who has knowledge of everything, past and future. When anyone reads the Qur'an with a sincere heart and an open mind, he sees that the models of people and societies described in the Qur'an existed in every age in history, including that of today, and that the Qur'an explains the current state of people and societies. All the disorder, perversion and mistakes of a society which has strayed from true religious values have been clearly stated in the Qur'an. The reactions of the people of these societies towards religion have been described with detailed character analyses. These descriptions and analyses are relevant in all respects to the world of today, thus demonstrating the "sociological miracle" of the Qur'an.

What is interesting here, is that such inconsistent views as: "Society is in a state of continuous progress, whereas religion is static" have also been diagnosed in the Qur'an as arising from a deficiency of comprehension. We should keep in mind that unbelievers, who lived thousands of years before the Qur'an, also interpreted religion as *"tales of the ancients"* (An-Nahl, 24)

When an individual starts reading the Qur'an and tries to implement it in his daily life, he can be considered to be on his way to becoming a real Muslim as described in the scriputures. With amazement, he begins to see how the Qur'an covers every moment of his life. Many events that a person experience have been mentioned in the Qur'an and the reactions of a Muslim which would befit those occasions have also been explained in detail.

Being satisfied with reading and knowing the Qur'an without practicing it, may have certain displeasing consequences. Allah describes the Jews as the kind of people who behave in this way and likens them to "a donkey which carries huge tomes" without any understanding of them:

> *"Those who were charged with the obligations of the Mosaic Law, but who subsequently failed in those obligations, are like a donkey which carries huge tomes without understanding them. Evil is the example of people who falsify the Signs of Allah: and Allah does not guide people who do wrong." (Al-Jumua, 5)*

RELIGION AS DESCRIBED IN THE QUR'AN AND THE RELIGION OF OUR FATHERS

∾

When they do anything that is shameful, they say: "We found our fathers doing so"; and "Allah commanded us thus": Say: "No, indeed, Allah never commands what is shameful: would you say of Allah what You do not, know?" (Al-Araf, 28)

It is impossible to imagine that true religion can exist wherever the Qur'an is abandoned. Therefore, a very clear distinction must be made between the religion of the Qur'an and those traditions which are wrongly considered to be a part of true religion.

The concept of religion requires special attention. Religion, that is, Islam, is purely and simply the implementation of the Qur'an. Whatever "religion" is considered to be nothing but a series of traditions handed down from the time of our forefathers is certainly not Islam.

Today, many people consider themselves religious, although they do not know much about the Qur'an. This shows us how the situation has deteriorated. Religion may continue to be a heritage from our forefathers, but trying to perpetuate such heritage has no value in the sight of Allah. In many societies where people are either Buddhists, Jewish or idolaters who live in an African clan and worship totems, they do what they do simply as a matter of tradition. Therefore, none of their practices amount to true religion. For most of the people following one of those "religions," the aim is not to seek the pleasure of Allah but, to try to live in conformity with society, satisfying their nostalgia by keeping their traditions alive and driving some personal interest from their religion.

Most people have developed a concept of religion, not by looking at its original sources, but by looking at their forefathers, so that their traditions of impressions about religion are, in fact, impressions about tradition.

As for tradition, it has a very large repertoire. This repertoire includes, many meaningless superstitions, invented stories, about saints false sayings and practices attributed to the prophets and the saints, unreasonable explanations of supernatural events, all of which are thought of as amounting to true religion.

In fact, many people who learn these traditions from their family and the society they live in, realize that these traditions stand on slippery ground and are full of countless sophistries. But because they do not want to put themselves out to search for the truth and the true nature of the religion, these people either choose to accept religion the way it is, or as mentioned in the beginning, stay away from it as far as possible. As a matter of fact, the very existence of those sophistries attributed to the true religion pave the way for justifying their escape from religion.

So, in order to understand the nature of true religion, what we should do in the first place is to refer to the Qur'an as a basic source of religion, ponder upon it and try to understand the scriptures as for as we are able. This is not something difficult to figure out. We should remember the fact that even non-believers directly refer to the Qur'an when they want to know something about Islam. Can you think of any better reference than the Qur'an as the original source of religion, which has been revealed by Allah to explain His divine system? Of course, certain other references should also be taken into account, but one should not forget that their actual value is to back up the Qur'an and lead us to refer to it in our attempts to understand religion.

People who build religion upon superstitions instead of the Qur'an are mentioned with disapproval;

> *"What is the matter with you that you should judge so ill?*
>
> *Or have you a book that promises you whatever you choose?" (Al-Qalam, 36-37)*

Religion should be the most important topic for a Muslim. He should know how to distinguish true religion from other systems, and should take as a duty the quest for the correct form of religion:

> *"...Now those who submit their wills - they have sought out the path of right conduct" (Al-Jinn, 14)*

TRUE BELIEVERS
AND IMPOSTORS
ᐁ

*Say: "To whom belong the earth and all beings
therein? Tell me, if you know!" They will say, "To
Allah!" Say: "Yet will you not receive admonition?"
Say: "Who is the Lord of the seven heavens, and the
Lord of the Throne (of Glory) Supreme?" They will
reply, "They belong to Allah." Say: "Will you not
then be filled with awe?" Say: "Who is it in whose
hands is the governance of all things,- who protects
all, but is not protected by anyone? Tell me, if you
know." They will say, Allah." Say: "Then how are
you deluded?" We have sent them the Truth: but they
indeed practise falsehood! (Al-Mumenoon ,84-90)*

Let's turn back to our example given in the beginning. We had
mentioned a group of people in the city, who were very
different from the others in every way, and towards whom all
other city dwellers had a hostile attitude. We had explained,
moreover, that, this group of people had a book which had
been conveyed to them by the Owner of that city and
everything else, as a guide. These people are called Muslim in
the Qur'an. They are the believers.

However, what we witness is that these people are not well-liked by the other people in the city. We had mentioned that the society of this city was a 'society of ignorance'. But, it does not mean that this society is irreligious. On the contrary, people of the society of ignorance consider themselves very religious people. However the religion they are associated with is not the true religion. It is a religion of tradition, a religion full of baseless and even perverted beliefs and practices which have their roots in the religion of their fathers. They think they follow the right religion and try to keep it alive with insistence. The Qur'an alludes to this characteristic in the following verse;

> *"When they are told to follow the Revelation that Allah has sent down, they say: 'No, we shall follow the ways that we found our fathers following'. What! Even if it is Satan beckoning them to the Penalty of the Blazing Fire?" (Luqman, 21)*

One of the most important characteristics of a society of ignorance is that its members defend their tradition in the name of Allah. As a matter of fact, this is an insincere defence for they are actually not concerned with Allah. While they–especially the leaders and the leading groups of the town–never stop praising Allah, they turn away from Him if religion conflicts with their interests — to the point of swearing by Allah even while committing the greatest offense of killing the Messenger.

> *"There were in the city nine men of a family, who made mischief in the land, and would not reform. They said: 'Swear a mutual oath by Allah that we shall make a secret night attack on him and his people, and that we shall then say to his heir when he seeks vengeance: We were not present at the slaughter of his people, and we are positively telling the truth."*
> *(Al-Naml, 48-49)*

There is also such a group in the society of ignorance who know the Qur'an and promise to follow its religion, but who prefer the "vanities of this world" and turn away from religion.

In spite of all this hypocrisy, they represent themselves as "perfect Muslims".

> *"After them succeeded an evil generation. They inherited the Book, but they chose for themselves the vanities of this world: saying Everything will be forgiven us.' And if similar vanities came their way, they would again indulge in them. Was not the covenant of the Book taken from them, that they would not ascribe to Allah anything but the truth? And they have studied what is in the Book. But best for the righteous is the home in the Hereafter. Will you not understand?" (Al-Araf, 169)*

In such as case, it takes more careful observation to understand if an individual or a group of people is truly Muslim or not. Because, as is clearly stated in the above verse, talking non-stop about religion does not necessarily show that the speaker is a real Muslim believer. One might think that such people hardly exist that they are very few in number. However, they are legion and in many verses of the Qur'an, their existence is openly mentioned.

> *"Of the people there are some who say: 'We believe in Allah and the Last Day? But they do not really believe.*
>
> *Vain would they deceive Allah and those who believe, but they only deceive themselves, and do not realize!*
>
> *In their hearts is a disease; and Allah has increased their disease: grievous is the penalty they will incur, because they are false to themselves." (Al-Baqara, 8-10)*

Other verses, warn us that when these "counterfeit religious people" are asked certain questions, they answer by "using the words of a believer."

> *"Say: 'Who is it that sustains you in life from the sky*

and from the earth? Who is it that has power over hearing and sight? And who is it that brings out the living from the dead and the dead from the living? Who is it that rules and regulates all affairs?' They will soon reply, 'Allah.' Say, 'Will you not then show piety to Him? Such is Allah, your real Cherisher and Sustainer: apart from truth, what remains but error? How then are you turned away?'" (Yunus, 31-32)

"If you ask them who created them, they will certainly say, 'Allah? How then are they diverted away from the Truth?" (Az-Zukhruf, 87)

All of these verses show us that the criterion for being a real believer is different from that "religious" criterion of a society of ignorance. In a society of ignorance, one who says, 'I'm a Muslim, alhamdulillah,' is considered to be a true Muslim. Yet when we consider the criterion of the Qur'an, we see that this is not adequate evidence. In the next chapter, we will be examining the characteristics of a true Muslim in detail.

BELIEVERS AS DESCRIBED IN THE QUR'AN
∾

True believers are those who, when Allah is mentioned, feel a tremor in their hearts, and when they hear His revelation, find their faith strengthened, and put all their trust in their Lord (Al-Anfal, 2)

... He has chosen you, and has imposed no difficulties on you in religion; it is the faith of your father Abraham. It is He Who has named you Muslims, both before and in this Revelation... (Al-Hajj, 78)

Who speaks better than one who calls men to Allah, does what is right, and says, "I am of those who bow in Islam"? (Fussilat, 33)

Islam has a single principle: worshipping only Allah. In Islam, the realization of this principle in life should be paramount. All other things not based on this principle are not Islam but some form of "religion of ignorance".

This reality expressed with such brevity, actually has a deeper meaning, much deeper, in fact than many people imagine. This is because the members of the society of ignorance already consider themselves believers and think of themselves as not worshipping anything other than Allah. And because they surely do not worship a statue while they are praying - an act which is usually performed exclusively at Bairams or on Fridays - then they imagine they have the right to think that they are worshipping only Allah.

However, the reality is quite other. This misapprehension arises from the fact that "worshipping" is understood only as prostrating oneself in front of a being that is to be served. This limited meaning of worshipping causes neglect of other religious duties and failure to adopt a Qur'anic morality. However, the real meaning of worshipping should be derived from the Qur'an. In other words, its meaning should be comprehended according to its description in the Qur'an, rather than its wrong portrayal by the society of ignorance.

> "I have created Jinns and men, only that they may serve Me." (Adh-Dhariyat 56)

As the above verse asserts, humans and Jinns are created to "serve Allah". It is certain that a believer is one who fits this definition. In accordance with his purpose of creation and his nature, a believer serves Allah alone, and, as mentioned in the verse, does nothing but worship Him. If we approach this verse with the understanding of the society of ignorance, should we conclude that a believer must stay in a position of self-prostration until the end of his life? Can this be the case?

Of course not. When we take a close look at the Qur'an, we see that worship of Allah includes all duties and responsibilities commanded in the Qur'an and all activities performed to gain the pleasure of Allah. How to serve Allah, and how to worship Him can be understood only by reference to the Qur'an:

> "Say: 'Truly, my prayer and my service of sacrifice, my life and my death, are all for Allah, the Cherisher of the Worlds.'" (Al-Anaam, 162)

As this verse indicates, the principle of worshipping Allah is not confined to praying, but overarches all of life and also death. A Muslim is one who spends all of his life in the way of Allah. As a result of this, he shall earn the good pleasure of Allah, His mercy and everlasting gardens in the hereafter–something that cannot be understood by anyone who is distant from Islam.

On the other hand, leading one's life to attain ends other than Allah's favour, is the same as "ascribing partners to Him", or in other words, "setting up partners with Him". These ends might be anything. They might be any desire to have wealth, a career, property, and women and sons, at the cost, as has been indicated in the Qur'an, of losing favour with Allah. When anyone so behaves giving a higher value to such objectives, in reality, he associates partners with Allah. This is the greatest sin one can commit. Throughout the ages, the prophets have urged people to stop attributing partners to Allah. The only purpose of these people in so doing was to come by different kinds of worldly gains. Bearing this in mind, one can also see how meaningless is the claim of dialectical materialism, which says that a process of evolution of polytheism to monotheism has taken place down the ages. According to the Qur'an, however, all societies of ignorance, which may exist at any time and at any place, have attributed partners to Allah. Consequently, today, a great part of the world population consists of the followers of some form of polytheistic religion. In this polytheistic world, exclusively, it is the societies of true believers who practice "the religion of worshipping only Allah".

> The only thing a believer must declare is: "Men! If you are in doubt as to my religion, behold! I do not worship what you worship, other than Allah! I worship Allah - Who will take your souls at the time of your death: I am commanded to be in the ranks of the Believers.'" (Yunus, 104)

Then, how should the believer worship Allah? How should he live his life in Allah's way? Should he go to spend all his life in a dervish lodge, or in a house of contemplation to undergo severe suffering through staying away from all worldly entities of life, including even those for survival? Or should he adopt a motionless, stable way of life as a withdrawn person? No. He is to live his life according to the model described in the Qur'an, not according to the definition of the religion concocted by the ignorant. Since he knows that Allah sees him, what other people think about him will trouble him. Since he knows he is not obliged to show himself as a religious person to others, he will not experience the distress of fulfilling the requirements of a false definition of the religious, which is not from the Qur'an.

He lives for Allah only, works only for Him. He misses no opportunity to use his capabilities, including his physical strength, in Allah's cause. This is not a way which is full of difficulties, or which deprives the invididual of all the pleasures of life, contrary to the belief of most people who do not know anything about Islam. Indeed, one who worships Allah is the most independent, the most peaceful, happy and cheerful. Once rid of all the fake deities which enslaved him, such questions as "What do people think about me?", "What can I do, if that person does not like me?", "What happens if I get fired?" No longer trouble him. Once rid of all the yokes laid upon him by those incapable, helpless, cruel, unreasonable gods, he can dedicate himself to the only God, the Mighty, the Wise, the knower of all things, the Compassionate, the Merciful and Powerful Allah. He "has grasped indeed the firmest hand to hold."

> "Let there be no compulsion in religion: Truth stands out clearly from Error: whoever rejects evil and believes in Allah has grasped the most trustworthy hand-hold, one that never breaks. Allah hears and knows all things." (Al-Baqara, 256)

The Qur'an thus expresses the Prophet's "freeing people from their chains and yokes":

*"Those who follow the Messenger, the Ummi, whom
they find mentioned in their own scriptures,- in the
law and the Gospel- he commands them to do what
is just and forbids them to do what is evil; he allows
them as lawful what is good and pure and prohibits
what is bad and impure; He releases them from their
heavy burdens and from the yokes that are upon
them. So it is those who believe in him, honour him,
help him, and follow the light which is sent down with
him, who will prosper."* (Al-Araf, 157)

Allah defines the believers as follows:

*"For Muslim men and women,- for believing men and
women, for devout men and women, for true men and
women, for men and women who are patient and
constant, for men and women who humble themselves,
for men and women who give in Charity, for men and
women who fast and deny themselves, for men and
women who guard their chastity, and for men and
women who engage much in Allah's praise,- for them
Allah has prepared forgiveness and a great reward."*
(Al-Ahzab, 35)

The Muslim has an intimate and close connection with
Allah. Allah is his only comrade, helper and God. The Prophet
Abraham's intimate liaison with Allah is made explicit in the
following dialogue with his father and his people:

*"He said: 'Do you then see whom you have been
worshipping, You and your fathers before you? For
they are enemies to me; not so the Lord and Cherisher
of the Worlds,*

Who created me; it is He Who guides me;

Who gives me food and drink,

And when I am ill, it is He Who cures me;

Who will cause me to die, and then bring me back to life again;

And Who, I hope, will forgive me my faults on the day of Judgment.

O my Lord! Bestow wisdom on me, and join me with the righteous Grant me honorable mention on the tongue of truth among the latest generations. Make me one of the inheritors of the Garden of Bliss. Forgive my father, for he is among those astray. Do not let me not be in disgrace on the Day when men will be raised up- the Day in which neither wealth nor sons will avail. " (Al-Shuara, 75-88)

The example of the comparison made between the person who feels the comfort of serving Allah only and the person who ascribes partners to God, and therefore serves too many gods, is given in the Qur'an as follows:

"Allah puts forth the parable of a man having many masters who are always at variance with each other, and a man belonging entirely to one master: are those two equal in comparison? Praise be to Allah! But most of them have no knowledge." (Az-Zumar, 29)

One of the most important characteristics of a believer is his avoidance of arrogance and haughtiness. A true believer never deifies himself. He knows his weaknesses and asks Allah to forgive him. He knows he needs to seek refuge with Allah in his every act, and in every part of his life. Because he is aware of his weaknesses, he does not have too high an opinion of himself. Therefore, he is not spiritually hampered by his self-created ego-boundaries and he improves himself with the help of Allah. He makes the effort to attain the believer model as described in the Qur'an. His humility can be seen in all his activities.

> *"And the servants of Allah, the Most Gracious, are*
> *those who walk on the earth in humility, and when*
> *the ignorant address them, they say, 'Peace!'"* *(Al-*
> *Furquan, 63)*

One of the biggest problem of a disbeliever is his being conceited, and deifying himself. The Qur'an asks us to consider the fate of those who reject the truth because of their conceit, although their souls confirm it:

> *"And they rejected those Signs in iniquity and*
> *arrogance, though their souls were convinced of their*
> *truth: so see what was the end of those who acted*
> *corruptly."* *(Al-Naml, 14)*

The believer's major purpose in life in this world is to struggle for his religion. He will fight against all the obstacles he encounters in Allah's cause. The biggest obstacle is the greediness and low desires of his soul, in other words his own self (nafs). All through his life, he will oppose his own self whenever it offers alternative which are against Allah's will. His own self will try to lead him astray turning him away from Allah's way by the use of countless tricks and obstacles such as fear, hopelessness, and slackness. However, a believer will overcome all of this through his eagerness, affection, determination, courage and patience. He will never digress from the right path because this is the path of Allah, his sole guardian, sole protector and sole supporter.

He does not struggle only for himself. He is the caliph of Allah on this earth, and the earth has been entrusted to him. Therefore, he will fight with wisdom against those transgressors who oppress people, tyrannize over them and try to prevent them from treading the path of Allah. In Qur'anic terms, he will bring Allah's salvation and justice to "those men, women and children who, being weak, are ill-treated and oppressed." The people on this earth will receive to Allah's justice through the efforts of these caliphs.

Only such societies as are governed by practitioner's of the moral principles and orders of the Qur'an can attain to real justice. A believer is one who deals with people justly and leads them to the truth for the pleasure of Allah. Those unbelievers who desire to govern society expect to obtain such worldly benefits as money, reputation and position; real justice can never be had during their period of leadership. But true believers shoulder the mission of 'practicing justice' all over the world. This is possible only by disseminating the morality of the Qur'an among people.

"Of those We have created those are some who direct others with truth. And dispense justice therewith."
(Al-Araf, 181)

The Qur'an also emphasizes the contrast between the believers and the mischief-makers on earth.

"Shall We treat those who believe and do deeds of righteousness, the same as those who create mischief on earth? Shall We treat those who guard against evil, the same as those who turn aside from the right?" (Sad, 28)

Believers struggle to save the world from calamity. The Qur'an indicates this strong characteristic of the believers as below.

Many of the prophets fought in Allah's way, and with them fought large bands of godly men? They never lost heart if they met with disaster on the path of Allah, nor did they weaken in will nor give in. And Allah loves those who are firm and steadfast. All that they said was: 'Our Lord! Forgive us our sins and anything We may have done that transgressed our duty: make us firm of foot and help us against those that resist Faith.' And Allah gave them a reward in this world, and the excellent reward of the Hereafter, for Allah Loves those who do good. O you who believe! If you obey the Unbelievers, they will drive you back on your heels, and you will turn back from Faith to your own loss." (Al Imran, 147-149)

A later verse from the same chapter shows how intrepid the true believers are:

> *"Men said to them: 'A great army is gathering against you: fear them,' But it only increased their Faith. They said: 'For us Allah suffices, and He is the best disposer of affairs.'" (Al Imran 173)*

A believer shoulders the mission of inviting people to Allah's religion. "Commanding what is just, and forbidding what is evil" is his foremost duty.

> *"True believers, men and women, are each others protectors: they enjoin what is just, and forbid what is evil: they say their regularly prayers, practice charity, without fail and obey Allah and His Messenger. On them will Allah pour His mercy: for Allah is Exalted in power, and Wise" (Al-Tawba, 71)*

One of the salient characteristics of a believer, which makes him different from the fake devotee, is that when he delivers the Qur'anic message to people, he does not expect to gain anything from it. His goal is not earning money, wealth and position, but the pleasure of Allah. He looks for his reward only on the path of Allah.

> *"But if you turn back, consider: no reward have I asked of you: my reward is only due from Allah, and I have been commanded to be of those who submit to Allah's will in Islam." (Jonah, 72)*

> *"Those were the prophets who received Allah's guidance: Follow the guidance they received and say: 'No reward for this do I ask of you. This is no less than a message for all the nations.'" (Al-Anaam, 90)*

The true believer is on an exalted plane of morality. He has an easygoing, tolerant, forgiving personality. Since he is not unduly swayed by events, he shows a mature reaction and behaves with wisdom, keeping his feelings well under control. He is self- sacrificing, helpful and kind.

> *"Those who patiently persevere, seeking the countenance of their Lord; say regular prayers; spend*

*out of the gifts. We have bestowed upon them for their
sustenance, secretly and openly; and ward off evil
with good: for such there is the final attainment of the
eternal home." (Al-Rad, 22)*

*A similar divine reward awaits those "who give alms
freely, whether in prosperity, or in adversity; who
restrain anger, and pardon all men;- for Allah loves
those who do good," (Al Imran, 134) who "hold to
forgiveness; command what is right; but turn away
from the ignorant," (Al-Araf, 199) and who "feed,
for the love of Allah, the indigent, the orphan, and
the captive" (Al-Insan, 8)*

Of course, the believer will make mistakes; after all he is
a human being. But as soon as he realizes his mistakes, he will
correct them and pray Allah to forgive his faults. None of his
faults make him hopeless, because he is sure of Allah's help and
seeks refuge in His boundless mercy. The Qur'an states this as
below:

*"And those who, having done something to be
ashamed of, or wronged their own souls, earnestly
bring Allah to mind, and ask for forgiveness for their
sins,—and who can forgive sins except Allah?—and
are never obstinate in persisting knowingly in the
wrong they have done." (Al Imran, 135)*

The believer's only friends are Allah and the servants of
Allah, other believers. He considers people only according to
their faith (imaan). He will not feel any affection for others
because of their race, career, family ties, or the profit he derives
from them. The only criterion which makes them worth his love
is their high degree of righteousness. His closest friend is no
longer a friend if he turns out to be an enemy to Allah. On the
other hand any believer who dedicates himself to Allah is a
close brother to him, even if they might not have nothing in
common in terms of a family relationship, social status or
financial opportunities. He likes for the pleasure of Allah, he

hates for the pleasure of Allah.

He is a man of understanding. He trusts in Allah. Because he puts his trust in Him, he is saved from fears, anxiety and sorrows of our worldly affairs. Since he is an "open-minded" person, he can think big and he can easily fathom the complex sides of events. His reason has been enforced by wisdom and knowledge.

He is a caliph on earth, who bears aloft the spirit of Allah. He is aware that he will be staying in this world for only a short time. During this short period, he will be tested and educated. Then he will be ready for his real home in the Hereafter. His life in this world is full of glory and honour as a caliph of Allah. No one can overcome him. They may kill him; yet this is the biggest reward for him, since this is by no means an end for him: being killed on the path of Allah is a great honour.

QUESTIONING
OURSELVES
ॐ

*O you who believe! Fear Allah, and let every soul look
to what provision He has sent forth for the morrow.
Yes, fear Allah: for Allah is well-acquainted with all
that you do. And do not be like those who forgot Allah
so that He made them forget their own souls! Such
are the rebellious transgressors! (Hashr, 18-19)*

The Qur'an describes the believers as explained in the previous
pages. The believers whom Allah is pleased with and whom
Allah allows into heaven, are such as are mentioned above. But
what about ourselves? Have we ever asked ourselves how
much we resemble them?

The model of the believer as described in the Qur'an shows
us that saying "alhamdulillah, I'm a Muslim" and performing
some simple acts of worship may not be enough in the eyes of
Allah. A true believer does not pay lip service but tries hard to
persevere in the way of Allah. The Qur'an explains the position
of those "serving Allah on the verge of true faith" as below:

> *"There are among men some who serve Allah, as it
> were, on the verge of true faith: if good fortune befalls*

them, they are well content; but if an ordeal befalls
them, they turn upon their heels: they lose both this
world and the Hereafter: that is a loss for all to see!"
(Al-Hajj, 11)

Another verse explains what is meant by worthy activities
in the path of Allah:

"It is not righteousness if you turn your faces towards
the east or west; but it is righteousness to believe in
Allah and the Last Day, and the Angels, and the
Book, and the Messengers; to spend your wealth, out
of love for Him, for your kin, for orphans, for the
needy, for the wayfarer, for those who ask, and for
the ransom of slaves; to be steadfast in prayer, and
practice regular charity; to fulfil the contracts which
you have made; and to be firm and patient, in
suffering and adversity, and throughout all periods
of panic. Such are the people of truth, the Allah-
fearing" (Al-Baqara, 177)

Obviously, it would be quite meaningless to deceive
ourselves by such thoughts as: 'My heart is pure, I do not have
any bad habits and I do not do any evil to anyone. Undoubtedly
Allah loves me'. Allah wants people to serve Him, and not just
be a pure-hearted person who does not do any harm to anyone.
No matter how pure one's heart is, if one does not obey the
commands of Allah and fulfill one's religious duties, one will
not please Allah. Besides, no one can have a pure heart without
true faith. Because, only true faith frees a person from such evils
as jealousy, passion for the world, selfishness, self-interest,
showing a lack of sympathy for others, etc. One should keep
in mind that these flaws cannot be removed from our souls
unless we are sedulous in our duties to Allah.

THE MODEL OF A PERSON LIVING IN A SOCIETY DISTANT FROM RELIGION

∾

They say: "What is there but our life in this world?
We live and die, and nothing but time can destroy
us." But of that they have no knowledge: they merely
conjecture. (Al-Jathiya, 24)

Yet there is among men such a one as disputes about
Allah, without Knowledge, without Guidance, and
without a Book of Enlightenment. (Al-Hajj, 8)

In spite of all these positive characteristics of the believers, there may still be people who are uninterested in religion. In order to understand the reason for this, we have to investigate their prejudices and impressions of Islam and Muslims. Here, we are not referring to atheists but to people who think they are Muslims without practicing the religion as required. The model meant here, is the model of so-called Muslims who live their lives according to certain principles that are not part of true religion. By the term "irreligious" we refer to those societies, people and/or principles having nothing to do with religion while not actually denying religion. Irreligious societies that are distant from true religious values are naturally made up of irreligious individuals. In fact, we are not entirely unfamiliar with this model at all, because it is actually a product of the society we are living in.

As we mentioned at the beginning, one of the most important characteristics of a person who fits into this model is his behaving in accordance with the conditioning of that society. All his manners are acquired by following the majority. This will also shape his point of view about religion.

All his religious thoughts are shaped by his environment. He has few opinions on the Qur'an, and maybe he has not read it even once in his life. Therefore, his only source of information about Islam and Muslims is the baseless practices of his grand parents and are just stories about Islam which are just hearsay. He thinks any activities carried out in the name of Islam, are a part of the real Islam.

At school, if his biology teacher is an evolutionist, or if his philosophy teacher is an atheist, he does not resist those ideas and readily accepts them to be true. He begins to think that he has been greatly enlightened. And he thinks he has found the truth and gone beyond the simple matters of life.

As mentioned before, section of the media try to show certain perverted persons as devotees and some perverted ideas as Islamic. They also represent believers as aggressive, fanatic, primitive, passive and isolated people. Through this systematic, discriminatory propaganda of the media, he thinks he has acquired an adequate knowledge of Islam. He is such a learned person that among his friends he does not hesitate to give expression off-the-cuff ideas and to make judgements about Islam. When he comes across his kind of men, the kind who agree with him, he gets even more sure of himself and of his ideas.

Wrong, distorted, unreasonable religious practices, which do not reflect the real Islam in any way, do not direct him towards searching for the truth. He does not bother to find out if there is actually a real religion. And after all why should he put himself out? He has more important things to attend to, such as school, work or taking care of his family. He does not want to accept the onus of discovering the reality. With the aid of materialistic media, he just suppresses the urgings of his soul to think about Allah and religion. Why should he bother to delve into the issue and further? If there is a system relating to Allah, which obligate people to practice it, how is he supposed to deal with his worldly matters? He wrongly thinks Islam will add to his troubles. His mind is so cloudy that he cannot even think that his escaping from reality will not free him from his responsibilities.

The situation of such people, who are in such a psychological state, is described in the following Qur'anic verse:

"Others they keep away from it, and themselves they keep away; but they only destroy their own souls, though they do not perceive it. (Al-Anaam, 26)

The irreligious attitude of the society in which he lives is his biggest support. The irreligious way of life adopted by members of "high society", politicians, writers and other famous and important persons, who are mostly known to be enlightened intellectuals, affects him deeply. After all, "high society" must go by the most appropriate norms of behaviour and he should be in conformity with the society he is living in.

By keeping away from religion, he thinks he becomes a modern and contemporary person. Being an irreligious person might make him feel guilty, but he comforts himself by thinking that there are many other people who share this guilt with him—as if this reduced the seriousness of his guilt. He thinks "committing an offense as a group reduces individual responsibility".

But, when he dies, he will be all alone. No one will be with him when he shall have to account for his actions. There won't be any help from those famous, enlightened people and members of high society:

*"They will all be marshalled before Allah together:
then the weak will say to those who were arrogant:
We but followed you; can you then protect us all from
the wrath of Allah?' They will reply, 'If we had
received the Guidance of Allah, we should have given
it to you: to us it makes no difference now whether
we rage, or bear these torments with patience: for
ourselves there is no way of escape.'" (Ibrahim, 21)*

*"And behold! You come to us bare and alone, as We
created you for the first time: you have left behind you
all the favours which We bestowed on you: We do not
see with you your intercessors whom you thought to
be partners in your affairs: so now all relations
between you have been cut off, and your fancies have
left you in the lurch!" (Al-Anaam, 94)*

Since he misunderstands the meaning of the concept of
'being elect', he takes wrong persons as models for himself.
According to the society of ignorance, to be an elect person,
some special qualifications are required, like possessing wealth
and fame. But these are irrelevant to Islamic criteria of
prominence. He is not aware of the fact that being an elect
person can be achieved only by being a pious believer who has
been brought near to Allah.

*"And commemorate Our Servants Abraham, Isaac,
and Jacob, possessors of Power and Vision. Truly, We
chose them for the special purpose of proclaiming the
Message of the Hereafter. They were, in Our sight,
truly, of the company of the Elect and the Good."
(Sad, 45-47)*

Society demands a great deal from him in terms of personal
qualifications and sacrifices. First of all, he needs to achieve
"status" and "prestige" in society in accordance with those
irreligious criteria. Otherwise, 'what will people think of him?'
Gradually, he learns more effective ways of "showing off" so
as to leave a "good" impression on people. For him, the only

thing that matters is "other peoples' impression of him". He is too preoccupied with how others think about him. And he does not seem to care about seeking the Good Pleasure of Allah. He claims to seek the pleasure of Allah, but when you look at his actions, you see that the only thing he cares about is currying favour.

Society also educates people about the nature of their relationship with the opposite sex. One of the most favourite slogans is "defend women's rights and show respect for women". But, in fact, women are used as an instrument of exploitation.

The logic of "dating with someone" is imposed as the only solution to certain social problems experienced by young people. This practice is encouraged without considering if it is an appropriate thing to do in terms of religious bounds. Term such as "flirt", "boy friend", "girl friend" and other similar experience have become standard items in the modern vocabulary. Young girls are given the 'holy' mission of satisfying the needs of men. Attempts are made to denigrate the concepts of honour and chastity through the systematic, hidden or open propaganda of the media, which become embedded in the subconscious. 13-14 year old girls can be labeled as "lesbian" if they do not have dates with boys. If a young man resists going to a brothel, he can also be labeled either as impotent or homosexual. Those who try to keep their chastity may find themselves isolated from society. In this way, social pressure is applied. If they do not act according to religion-free social rules, public opinion will compel them to change their ways and in the face of this pressure their self-discipline crumble.

Thus conditioned, the young person starts to see sexual relationships outside marriage as lawful. Next comes the shaping of our views about homosexuals. With systematic propaganda the ordinary man is induced to believe in the normality of homosexuality: "Being a homosexual is a personal choice, which should be considered very natural." When you consider it normal, you are considered to be an open-minded, modern and notable person. In order to be such a person, you have to overcome your "old-fashioned" way of thinking and "improve" yourself. The more you accept any sort of "immorality" as legitimate, the more you become a "modern", "notable" person! Who can resist becoming such a person? In fact, a true believer does!

Let's take a further look at some other characteristics of this system. It uses "marriage" —originally an institution of mutual respect and love with no expectation of profit as an instrument of mutual exploitation. In this system, the role of a wife is rearing the children, washing the clothes and dishes, cooking and providing sexual satisfaction for her husband. After "finding a husband" one of the most important goals for a young girl, she tries to "bind" her husband to herself by having a child as soon as possible in order to "guarantee" her future. The role of a husband, on the other hand, is working for a living and earning money for his "dearest" wife's needs in payment for her "services". This is nothing but a mutual life contract based on personal interests and social rules. This kind of marriage is not actually very different from an agreement made for any kind of temporary service. The only difference is in the duration of the validity of the agreement. This marriage is calculated to last for a longer time, maybe for a lifetime. Neither partner want to accept this truth, but when they see there is no love and respect in their relationship, but only role playing, they admit the true nature of their marriage to be a "reality of life". When one spouse reneges on fulfilling his/her duties as this agreement requires, their marriage shatters.

There is the concept of "marriage by logic." It means that couples may get married if certain standards are met by the two parties, although love and sincere intimacy are not involved. Love is something temporary anyway and it is to die sooner or later. So, there's no need to be in love with the person you marry. As may easily be understood, in this kind of marriages the common sharing point is not love, but money, and mutual benefits. Even sexuality, after a period of time, is considered to be a boring act, since spouses get used to each other. And even love has a distorted meaning when it is involved in the relationship. It is based on certain materialistic criteria. Young girls easily fall in love with those "cool guys" with "red sports cars". Their being irreligious person does not really matter. Since no morality as described in true religion is involved, the ensuing rooted in iniquity.

It is obvious that in these marriages, concepts such as loyalty and fidelity do not have any importance. The increasing number of cheating partners is a natural result of this system. They begin to cheat on each other after a period of time and many of them maintain their forbidden relationships secretly. Some "modern" people, on the other hand, do this within the knowledge of their spouses, and are proud of their "honesty" towards them. The "modern marriage system", which is entirely different from the one described in Islam, is promoted and shown to be the ideal one. This system is used as a doorway to "free sex", widely practiced by certain "modern" groups of society, who are doing their utmost to make this a permanent concept.

Actually, the irreligious way of life, introduced as modernism, is not an independent philosophy at all. It is a thought system which is promoted to destroy religious values and to establish a social system in opposition to them. It has the effect of preventing people from carrying out their religious duties. The rules of this thought system apply not only to marriage but also to many aspects of life. The system either attempts to destroy certain concepts like chastity and loyalty, or distort the meaning of others incorporating them in its own system in order to mislead people. Characteristics like honesty, courage, and being brave in the way of Allah are some of those virtues which are highly praised in the Qur'an. Fighting against the unjust, determination to the extent of sacrificing one's life in the way of Allah, fearing nothing but Allah are also among the most important characteristics of the believers. But this system describes courage as indulging in the most extreme perversions, honesty as engaging openly in immoral activities, and determination as being firm in maintaining and promoting one's irreligious values.

When we look at the situation of youngsters, we see that such concepts as "courage" and "decisiveness" are associated with   certain personality distortions like rudeness, disrespectfulness, bullying, attacking human rights, being opportunist, abusing people, aggressiveness, arrogance and overestimating oneself. The "rebel", the "tough guy" and the "macho guy" are represented to youngsters as if these were ideal personality types. Indiscreetness and garrulity are praised as signs of being a "straightforward" person.

Allah warns us about the untrustworthiness of people with the above mentioned characteristics.

> "Do not heed such a despicable type of person as is ready with oaths, a slanderer, spreading calumnies, Habitually hindering all good, transgressing beyond all bounds, deep in sin, violent and cruel and with all that, base-born. Though he may possess wealth and numerous sons, when our revelations are recited to him, he cries 'Tales of the ancients', !" (Al-Qualam, 10-15)

For a young girl, having free sex and defending lesbianism are represented as acts of "courage", and confessing her unfaithfulness to her husband is regarded as a mark of "honesty". "Respect" is a feeling of appreciation which has to be shown for all kinds of perversions.

As a consequence of all this distorted logic, the concept of "loving someone" takes on a different meaning. The degree of love is in direct proportion to how much one can show off in the relationship and how much material benefit one can derive from it. Love is based on certain deliberately created images. Many young girls fall for a 'romantic rebel' only because of his image. Under the influence of this image factor, they look with sympathy upon people, who are really quite ordinary and possess very few qualities. On the other hand, they are ready to criticize those devoted, respectful believers with many praiseworthy traits, if they mistakenly commit even the slightest error. While the image of being a believer has a little value, the useless rebel quite bereft of positive characteristics, attracts much more attention.

The society the individual lives in, forms his value-judgement and shapes his thoughts and feelings to such an extent that he eventually gives no thought to the purpose of life, his existence, religion and Allah. Since the system imposes countless duties upon him, he has in any case, no time to think on such issues. First of all, he needs to be the captain who saves his ship, thus earning his status in society. In order to reach this goal, he shall have to manipulate and abuse people.

Life is a struggle. Big fish swallow smaller fish. Elimination of the weak is a "law of nature". So he must play the game accordance to his own rules. He does not care about others having the same mentality, so long as they do not use it against him.

But once things do not work out as he plans and he fails in his attempts to gain some "status" in society, the mentality he favoured so far, turns out to be a threat to his existence. He finds himself in the ranks of those upon whom he used to look down. His so-called friends, who in fact did not care about him but only about what he seemed to be till that point, now disappear one by one and leave him all alone. Once he loses his business, wealth, health and status, or anything considered to be one of the main criteria for love or give loving anyone or giving him any importance, all friends turn away from him. He now sees that it is only Allah he can trust and ask for help. It is only Allah in whom he can seek refuge.

It is the Who enables them to traverse the land and sea; they embark and set sail with a favourable wind, at which they rejoice; then comes a stormy wind and the waves come to them from all sides, and they think they are being overwhelmed: they pray to Allah, with all fervor saying, 'If you deliver us from this, we shall truly show our gratitude!'" (Jonah, 22)

But as soon as Allah answers his prayers and things start to go well for him, like those whom Allah delivered from being shipwrecked, he again turns away from Allah, as if he was not the one who desperately asked for help and promised to be a true servant if his prayers were answered.

> *"But when he delivers them, behold! They transgress insolently throughout the earth in defiance of right! O mankind! Your insolence is against your own souls. Take your enjoyment of the life of the present but in the end, to Us you shall return, and We shall show you the truth of all that you did." (Jonah, 23)*

He again starts to evaluate things with his distorted materialistic mentality. He considers what he has been through as a mere experience of life and claims he was saved from that undesirable situation through his own efforts. Things should be considered realistically, not in terms of religion or metaphysics. Everything is over anyway. Now it is time to return to the game. This time he will be more careful to play it by his own rules. After all, he is now more experienced.

> *"If We give man a taste of Our Mercy, and then withdraw it from him, behold! He is in despair and falls to blaspheming. But if We give him a taste of Our favours after adversity has touched him, he is sure to say, 'All evil has departed from me' and behold! He becomes exultant and boastful." (Hud, 9-10)*

His devianic is now more firmly established. During the rest of his life, he will be tested and he will encounter similar troubles again. These will all provide new opportunities for him to turn to Allah. And it would be good for him if he learnt his lesson and found the straight path with the aid of Allah. But if he resists and turns away, these chances will only cause his deviance to become the more ingrained.

The worst of all is, if his life ends before he sees the warning in these tests and carries out his duties to Allah. Then it will be too late, because he has been given enough chances and he has already proven what kind of a person he has been during his lifetime. He has used up all his chances. The situation of such people is stated in the Qur'an as follows;

> "If you could only see them they are confronted with the Fire! They will say: 'Would that we were but sent back! Then we would not reject the signs of our Lord, but would be amongst those who believe!' Indeed, what they concealed before will become manifest to them. But if they were sent back, they would certainly return to the things they were forbidden, for they are indeed liars." (Al-Anaam, 27-28)

In other verses of the Qur'an, the unbelievers' similar position is emphasized and they are advised to turn to Allah during their lifetime in this world.

> "For any whom Allah leaves astray, there is no protector thereafter. And you will see the Wrong-doers, when in sight of the Penalty, say: 'Is there any way to effect a return?'

And you will see them brought forward to the Penalty, in a humble frame of mind because of their disgrace, and looking with a stealthy glance. And the Believers will say: 'Great indeed is the loss of those who have given to perdition their own souls and all their kindred on the Day of Judgment.' Truly, the wrong-doers shall suffer everlasting torment; And they have no protectors to help them, other than Allah. And for any whom Allah leaves to stray, there is no way to the Goal.

> Obey your Lord, before there comes a Day which no one can put off against the will of Allah! That Day there will be no place of refuge for you nor will there be any room for denial of your sins!" (Al-Shura, 44-47)

TRANSITION TO QUR'ANIC MORALITY FROM THAT OF THE IRRELIGIOUS SOCIETY

ॐ

But if any have done wrong and have thereafter substituted good to take the place of evil, truly, I am Oft-Forgiving and Most Merciful. (Al-Naml, 11)

And thus have We, by Our Command, sent inspiration to you: when you knew nothing of Revelation or Faith; but We have made the Qur'an a Light, wherewith We guide such of Our servants as We will; and surely you will guide men to the Straight Way. (Al-Shura, 52)

For they have been guided (in this life) to the purest of speeches; they have been guided to the Path of Him Who is Worthy of (all) Praise. (Al-Hajj, 24)

Every person, throughout his life, has a chance of getting rid of what society has instilled in him and turning to Allah's way. According to the way of Allah, no one will depart from this world before he is invited to the religion of Allah by a Warner. Every person who is responsible for his acts, will be invited to

Islam and he will be asked to make a choice of his free will.

> *"Whoever receives guidance, receives it for his own benefit: but whoever goes astray does so to his own loss. No bearer of burdens can bear the burden of another: nor do We punish a native until We have sent a messenger to give warning." (Al-Isra, 15)*

Those who receive this invitation, give different responses. The Qur'an explains their reaction in detail. The best reaction is that of the real Believers when they express their acceptance by saying, "We hear and we obey."

> *"The answer of the Believers, when summoned to Allah and His Messenger, in order that He may judge between them, is no other than this: they say, 'We hear and we obey': it is such as these that will attain felicity." (Al-Nur, 51)*

Nevertheless not everybody's reaction is as ideal as this. The Qur'an also mentions those who deny their religion with pride and even hold Muslims as enemies, when they are invited to accept what Allah has revealed.

> *"Woe to each sinful dealer in falsehoods! He hears the Signs of Allah recited to him, yet is obstinate and lofty, as if he had not heard them: then announce to him a grievous penalty!: When he learns something of Our Signs, he takes them in jest: for such there will be a humiliating penalty." (Al-Jathiya, 7-9)*

Others, on the other hand, are more ambiguous in their reactions The soul of such individual tells him what is right and wrong, but another, inner voice keeps on instilling in him the determination not to turn away from the irreligious society. He tries to make this legitimate through by defense mechanisms. He tries in several ways to escape from reality. Since he cannot say, "Believers are telling me the truth, but I do not accept and practice what they tell me to do because of my own weakness and pride," he tries to find faults in religion itself and in the believers in order to reassure to comfort himself.

When such a person meets a true believer who is sincere towards Allah, he approaches him with suspicion and prejudice. When he sees that this believer is not of the "traditional" mould, he claims him to be a person who "is interpreting religion according to his own desires and using religion for his own benefit." What is interesting is that this accusation has even been directed against the prophets;

> *"The unbelieving elders of his people said: 'He is no more than a man like yourselves: his wish is to assert his superiority over you: if Allah had wished to send messengers, He could have sent down angels; never did we hear such a thing as he says, among our ancestors of old.'" (Al-Mumenoon, 24)*

> *"Would you now forbid us to worship the gods our fathers worshipped? But we are really in serious doubt as to the faith to which you call us." (Hud, 62)*

All of a sudden, he decides to be a great voluntary defender of the distorted understanding of the religion of ignorance. He objects to the way believers live, since they have given up the distortions of religion which stem from the wrong practices of their ancestors, and have been living out their religion as defined in the Qur'an. He asks the real Muslim: "What is it that you claim? That everyone is doing wrong, and only you are doing right,? "Are you the only ones who happened to realize the true meaning of religion?" "You claim you are wiser than most of the believers on earth and have found the true way?" However, according to the Qur'an, the truth is not measured by the number of people who believe it to be true. On the contrary, the Qur'an warns us that most of the people will not be on the right path:

> *"...These are the signs (or verses) of the Book: that which has been revealed to you from you Lord is the Truth; but most men do not believe. (Al-Rad, 1)*

While some of the prophets had a numerous following (like the Prophet Moses,   the Prophet Solomon, the Prophet Mohammed), other prophets were followed only by a small number of believers and sometimes not even by a single person, as is mentioned in the Qur'an. However, the number of the believers did not change the reality, and all prophets conveyed Allah's message to their people. They fulfilled their duties and were rewarded with the highest gardens in the hereafter, regardless of the number of believers that followed them.

The Qur'an clarifies the position of the people who interrogate the believers, making distorted inferences;

> *"Do you not see those who turn in friendship to people with whom Allah is angry? They belong neither to you nor to them, and they swear to falsehood knowingly." (Al-Mujadila, 14)*

> *"(They are) distracted in mind being sincerely for neither one group nor for another. Allah leaves them straying,- never will you find the way." (An-Nisa, 143)*

This kind of person tries to find deficiencies in the explanations of the real religion based on the Qur'an. Although he does not know much about the Qur'an, he enters into disputes and produces examples to defend his distorted logic. (These examples are called "comparisons" by the Qur'an) In fact, his claims are quite baseless and without consistency, and are put forward as a way of escape.

> *"See what kinds of epithets they bestow on you! But they have gone astray, and never will they be able to find the true path!" (Al-Furqan, 9)*

The best-known comparisons do not exceed four or five. For example, "Why is the eating of the flesh of swine forbidden by religion?" Is one of the most frequent questions asked. The person who asks this question is well aware that swine feeds on its own excreta, causes a parasite disease and is therefore harmful to human health. He nevertheless feels disgusted when these facts are mentioned. However, his actual aim is not to get some reasonable answer but to confuse minds. The fate of such people is described in the Qur'an:

> "But those who strive against Our Signs, to frustrate them,- they will be Companions of the Fire." (Al-Hajj, 51)

> "Those who would hinder men from the path of Allah and would seek in it something crooked: it was they who denied the Hereafter!" (Hud, 19)

Even if these comparisons are proven to be nonsense, further comparisons are made up instantly, since the real aim is not to be informed or have suspicions allayed but to search for deficiencies. If he considers the given answers with a sincere heart, he will be convinced and have to accepted how reasonable they are. However, he avoids this. Because he does not want to make a change in his plans and in his way of life to conform to a new set of criteria. As a result, he thrusts his fingers into his ears so as not to hear the reality as it is explained in the Qur'an;

> "And every time I have called on them, to seek your pardon, they have only thrust their fingers into their ears, covered themselves up with their garments, grown obstinate, and given themselves up to arrogance" (Nooh, 7)

Those who refuse to accept advice are compared with asses:

> "Then what is the matter with them that they turn away from admonition?- As if they were frightened asses, fleeing from a lion!" (Al-Muddaththir, 49-51)

We are again informed by the Qur'an that those people who turn away from Islam, hiding behind primitive reactions, excuses and distortions are described as wrong-doers and unjust:

"Who does greater wrong than one who invents a falsehood against Allah, even as he is being called to Islam? Allah does not guide those who do wrong." (As-Saff ,7)

If he is shrewd, he takes this invitation as a challenge and tries to prove his "vigilance" and "shrewdness". Nobody can "dupe" him after all. He approaches Muslims in a paranoid and hostile manner. Since he thinks people are keenly attentive only to their own interest only, just like himself, he cannot understand the sincere and self-sacrificing efforts of Muslims for the cause of Allah. He tries to explain the unity and solidarity of believers by putting forward ignorant points of view. "There is something behind all this," he says and he thinks that by being suspicious, he is being wise.

"When they meet those who believe, they say: 'We believe' but when they are alone with their evil ones, they say: 'We are really with you: we were only jesting.' Allah will throw back their mockery on them, and give them rope in their trespasses; so that they will wander like the blind." (Baqara, 14-15)

In fact, his insincere, prejudiced, hostile manners towards Muslims are not a unique attitude disorder special to himself. Historically, all ignorant people have used the very same tactics and acted in the same manner. Throughout the ages, mentality, methods and comparisons have remained unchanged.

"On the contrary, they say things similar to what the ancients said." (Al-Mumenoon, 81)

They either reject revelations or try to distort their meaning to make them serve their own interests. They suggest criteria other than those included in the Qur'an.

"What is the matter with you that you judge so ill?

Or have you a book through which you learn-that you shall have, through it, whatever you choose?

Or have we sworn a covenant with you —binding till the Day of Judgment,—that you shall have whatever you shall demand?" (Al-Qalam, 36-39)

When he numbers among the ignorant, he hardly remembers his being a Muslim. He never considers whether or not his actions, attitudes, relationships with others, or his way of life conform to Qur'anic criteria. However, when he meets a sincere Muslim, he suddenly remembers that he is a Muslim. And what is more, that he is a "very" religious one. He starts uttering clichés to prove how religious a person he is. "I am a Muslim, alhamdulillah" "I never skip prayers at eids" " I never use alcohol while fasting in the month Ramadan". Statements of this kind are in fact reflections of his psychological state as he tries to hide his real personality.

Some "shrewd" people go a step further and act as if they were the most religious of all. They compare themselves with those who engage in distorted forms of religion and declare, "My heart is pure, I am a more religious person than most of those religious-looking people." They say, "Allah knows who is on the right path" and object to other people making any comment on their irreligious way of life, no matter how openly they are involved in unlawful activities like "usury" and "adultery". Surely Allah knows who are on the right path and who are not, but He guides us to the right path by stating in the Qur'an that being a true believer is only possible by being in possession of the characteristics of the believers as explained in the Qur'an. As the criteria of the Qur'an are very clear, a one who claims superiority for himself without having any knowledge of the Qur'an does nothing but dishonour himself.

One of the biggest errors of such people is that they wrongly assume that they can deceive others. However, real believers can easily diagnose such people, with their understanding and the ability given by Allah together with the knowledge provided by the Qur'an. Besides, Allah, Who "knows well all the secrets of the heart" (Al Imran, 119) sees them and knows them better than they do themselves. Such people believe that they can deceive Allah just as they deceive other people. On the Day of Judgement, no excuses from them will be accepted before Allah.

THE WORLD AND
THE HEREAFTER

ဢ

Fair in the eyes of men is the love of things they covet: women and sons; heaped-up hoards of gold and silver; horses branded (for blood and excellence); and (wealth of) cattle and well-tilled land. Such are the possessions of this world's life; but in nearness to Allah is the best of the goals.

> Say: "Shall I give you glad tidings of things far better than those? For the righteous are Gardens in close proximity to their Lord, with rivers flowing beneath; therein is their eternal home; with companions pure and holy; and the good pleasure of Allah." Allah is watching over His servants. (Al Imran, 14-15)

Essentially all attempts to seek in religion something crooked, stem from a lack of understanding of the reality of the Hereafter.

As is stated in the Qur'an, Allah has created the World as a temporary home for us. It is for putting believers to the test, having them purified, letting them become worthy of heaven and bearing witness against the unbelievers.

However, members of the society of ignorance disregard this reality and hold on to the World alone as if it will never end. That is the reasoning that shapes the mentality of the society of ignorance which we have tried to explain throughout this book. "Life is short, so get a life", "We come to this world only once, so enjoy it." Statements of this kind are actually simple reflections of this mentality which urge people to live their lives without considering their religious duties and the hereafter. You should enjoy your life while you are alive. You can try anything for fun and for your benefit because in the society of ignorance, as long as you benefit from something, there is nothing wrong with it. From that standpoint, everything is legitimate.

The society of ignorance is in a state of deep ignorance. It is clear that death is an unavoidable end and that it will come sooner or later to everyone on earth. Yet, the ignorant disregard this fact and keep it out of the agenda as much as possible. They sedulously avoid thinking about it and prevent people from talking about it. Everybody leads his life as if he will never die, although most people do not deny the existence of Allah. When they are asked, they claim they do believe in the afterlife as well, as it is a prerequisite of being a Muslim. However, their actions prove just the opposite. That is because of their lack of faith in the hereafter:

> "As to these, they love the fleeting life, and put away behind them a Day that will be hard." (Al-Insan, 27)

> "You will indeed find them, of all people, most greedy of life,-even more than the idolaters: Each one of them wishes He could be given a life of a thousand years: but the grant of such life will not save him from (due) punishment. For Allah sees well all that they do." (Al-Baqara, 96)

> "Ah indeed! Are they in doubt concerning the Meeting with their Lord? Ah indeed! It is He that doth encompasses all things!" (Fussilat, 54)

Since they think their death will be an ultimate end for their being, their desire to live forever is fulfilled in another way. Most of the ignorant want to leave behind them something to make people remember them after their death. They think, by doing so, they will be living in people's minds. They are unaware of how unreasonable this way of thinking is. Instead of doing some good deeds for their afterlife, they try to make a "name" for themselves in the world so as to be "unforgettable" after their death, none of which activity will bring them any benefit.

> *"Behold, their brother Hud said to them: 'Will you not fear Allah?*
>
> *I am to you a messenger worthy of all trust:*
>
> *So fear Allah and obey me. I ask no reward of you for it: my reward is only from the Lord of the Worlds.*
>
> *Do you build a landmark on every high place to amuse yourselves?*
>
> *And do you raise up for yourselves fine buildings in the hope of living in them for ever?'"* (Al-Shuara, 124-129)
>
> *"......who piles up wealth and lays it by, thinking that his wealth would make him last for ever!"* (Al-Humaza, 2-3)

Belief in the Hereafter is a kind of consolation to repress the pain death causes during the life of this world. Even the most religious ones make superstition of it. They choose to believe in it "just in case". They believe they guarantee their entry to the Gardens in the hereafter. What is interesting is that those who approach the hereafter in such a way, claim that they are "people of the Gardens." The person mentioned in the chapter Al-Kahf symbolizes this general point of view of the society of ignorance:

> *"Set forth to them the parable of two men: for one of them We provided two gardens of grape-vines and*

*surrounded them with date palms; in between the two
We placed corn-fields.*

*Each of those gardens brought forth its produce, and
did not fail in the least therein: in the midst of them
We caused a river to flow.*

*When their ones had gathered in his harvest, he said
to his companion, in the course of a mutual argument:
'I have more wealth than you, and more honour and
power in my following of men.*

*He went into his garden in a state of mind unjust to
his soul. He said, 'Surely this will never perish!*

*Nor do I believe that the Hour of Judgment will ever
come: Even if I am brought back to my Lord, I shall
surely find there something better in exchange.'*

*His companion said to him, in the course of the
argument with him: 'Do you deny Him Who created
you out of dust, then out of a sperm-drop, then
fashioned you into a man?*

*I think for my part that He is Allah, My Lord. and
none shall I associate with my Lord.*

*Why did you not, as you went into your garden, say:
'Allah's will be done! There is no power but with
Allah!' If you see me less than you in wealth and sons,
it may be that my Lord will give me something better
than your garden, and that He will send down on
your garden thunderbolts by way of reckoning from
heaven, making it but slippery sand!*

*Or the water of the garden will run off underground
so that you will never be able to find it.'*

So his fruits (and enjoyment) were destroyed, and he wrung his hands over all that he had spent on his property, which had now tumbled to pieces to its very foundations, and he could only say, 'Woe is me! Would that I had never ascribed partners to my Lord and Cherisher!'

He had no one to help him against Allah, nor was he able to deliver himself.

In such ordeals the only protection comes from Allah, the True One. He is the Best to reward, and the Best to give success." (Al-Kahf, 32-44)

In another chapter of the Qur'an, we see another example of a person with such a mentality. When he says "If I am brought back to my Lord." He, in fact, confesses his disbelief in the hereafter;

"When we give him a taste of our Mercy after some adversity has touched him, he is sure to say, 'This is due to my own merit: I do not think that the Hour of Judgment will ever come; but if I am brought back to my Lord, He will surely reward me well. But We will show the Unbelievers the truth of all that they did, and We shall give them the taste of a severe Penalty." (Fussilat, 50)

It is in fact hard to understand why people of the society of ignorance persist in their blindness. If someone believes in Allah, then he inevitably comes to the conclusion that the hereafter must also exist. Allah creates the human being, lets him live his life, gives him countless blessings and shows him great compassion and mercy. So, why should He want to annihilate him at a certain age?

Let s remember an example given by a great Islamic scholar on this subject: Can a mother execute her child after bringing him up all through the years? In fact, a mother cares a lot about her child and she feels a great deal of compassion towards him. She does not even think about doing him any harm, let alone wanting him. When these feelings have been given to her by Allah as the ultimate owner of compassion and any concept we know of good, how can anyone believe that Allah annihilates the human beings whom He creates and endows with all kinds of blessings, especially when those people are thankful to Him and choose to be His servants?

Perhaps we could have a reason to think that death was an end, if good people lived endlessly on the earth while evil ones died. However, as mentioned in the verse: "Every soul shall have a taste of death" (Al-Anbiya 35) Allah ends one's life after allowing him to live for a certain period of time. "Did We not give you long enough life so that he that would should receive admonition? And (moreover) the warner came to you." (Al-Fatr, 37) This period of time is sufficient for each one of us to make a choice.

During this period of time, people should realize that their souls are immortal. Allah has made us want various things and He has given us all that we want and need. Allah has created us in such a way that we feel hunger and He has bestowe upon us in plenty the foods of the earth. Having given us the feeling of thirst He created water resources for humans when he created the earth. Then, in the same way, will not Allah let us live forever, as He has made us desire to live forever? Allah has created the human being as His caliph on the earth and pressed all other created things, like the sun, the stars and the earth into his service. After all that perfect creation on the part of Allah, it would be unreasonable to think that He allows mankind to live on the earth for a period of time and then ends his life forever. In short, when we pass away, we do not become lost in "nothingness", but step into our real lives.

It is very obvious to the thinking person that life in this world is temporary and simply a sample of the real life. All the beauties in the world are temporary and have many deficiencies. The most good-looking human being can keep his good appearance only for one or two decades. As he gets older and older, his physical appearance changes, his skin becomes puckered, his body loses its shape and he starts to suffer many kinds of illnesses related to aging. It is not necessary to get older to witness the shortcomings of the life of this world. His body mechanisms are built with many weaknesses. If he does not take a shower for a few days, he starts to stink. No matter how attractive he is, he has to use the lavatory as every human being does and has to deal with this kind of weaknesses in himself every single day all through out his life.

Since people are used to all of this, they are usually not aware that these weaknesses have been given to them on purpose. They consider the presence of these weaknesses very normal and never think that there could be any alternative. However, Allah's creation is perfect. When we look at the creation of the universe, the earth, nature and all living creatures from complex organisms to single celled structures, we clearly see that there is a perfect order and design in everything. So, if Allah had willed, people would not have had any of the above mentioned. But all these deficiencies are to remind people of the fact that they stand in need of Allah. They are also to remind people that, the life in this world is only an example of the real life in the hereafter, which is free of all deficiencies.

> "Know that the life of this world is but play and amusement, pomp and mutual boasting and multiplying, in rivalry among yourselves, riches and children. It is like the plants that flourish after rain, delighting the hearts of the tillers; but soon they withers; you will see them grow yellow; then become dry and crumble away. But in the Hereafter there is as severe Penalty for the devotees of wrong. And Forgiveness from Allah and His Good Pleasure for the devotees of Allah. And what is the life of this world, but the goods and chattels of deception?" (Al-Hadid, 20)

Then, one may ask, "What is the real life like?" It is known to all that, there will be two different abodes in the hereafter, one for the believers, Paradise, and the other for the unbelievers, Hell. However, the society of ignorance has not stopped short of producing tales about Paradise, and Hell. Therefore, we again need to refer to the Qur'an to understand the true nature of the hereafter.

PARADISE :
REAL HOME OF THE
BELIEVERS

ॐ

*Be foremost in seeking Forgiveness from your Lord,
and a Garden of Bliss, as vast as heaven and earth,
prepared for those who believe in Aliah and His
messengers: that is the Grace of Allah, which He
bestows on whom he pleases: and Allah is the Lord
of Grace abounding. (Al-Hadid, 21)*

*There will be for them therein all that they wish,- and
more besides in Our Presence. (Qaf, 35)*

The eternal home of the believers is Paradise. Allah will reward
them by leading them into the gardens, where they will dwell
forever. Paradise is a place where believers will find whatever
they want and even more than what they want, for the beauties
of Paradise are beyond their imagination.

Yet the common perception of Paradise is significantly
different from what is described in the Qur'an. According to
the traditional point of view, Paradise is an improved version
of the East, especially where Arab culture prevailed, again,

according to this view, Paradise is a place lacking technology place where people mostly enjoy its natural beauties, trees, streams, etc. As to the chalets of Paradise, they are thought to be similar to those chalets of 17th century Middle Eastern Culture, Ottoman culture for example. People usually visualize clothing in Paradise to be a somewhat modernized version of baggy trousers, robes in religious style and turban. They imagine a "houri" whose beauty is highly praised in the Qur'an, to be very beautiful, yet their conception of this beauty is limited to the standards of traditional Ottoman harems, or to some other standards, depending on the country they are from, or the cultural background they have.

All these wrong assumptions stem from the flawed mentality of those who consider the eastern world as a creation of Allah and the western world as something apart from His creation. While they try to avoid certain low moral standards of the western world, they also try to ignore its good parts, as if the technology, luxury and western style of aesthetics were not owned by Allah; Who is the owner of everything. What this twisted logic claims, in fact, is that Allah exists in Mecca but not in Los Angeles. Even most of the Muslims who live in the western world are convinced that Paradise will be in oriental style.

The reality is not like that, however? "...Allah has power over all things, encompassing all things in His Knowledge." (Al-Talaq, 12) and He is "...the Lord of all points in the East and the West." (Al-Maarij, 40) So, Paradise cannot be bereft of any of the beauties of this world, regardless of whether they belong to the East or to the West. Otherwise, Paradise would not be Paradise. The houses in Paradise will be much better than the most beautiful palaces of this world. The praised beauties of paradisiacal garments will be much more elegant and aesthetic than those of French or Italian fashion houses. The women in Paradise will not necessarily look like oriental dancers but they will be much more beautiful and attractive than any of the top models and cover girls, since their beauty as described in the Qur'an and Islamic literature is unparalleled.

Not all Islamic concepts are necessarily oriental. When anyone reads the Qur'an without giving it close attention, he may first get an impression that technology does not exist in the gardens of Paradise. That is because the Qur'an which was revealed 1400 years ago, describes Paradise in such a way as can be understood by people of all ages. Then Qur'an is universal and applies to all ages. It does not, of course, "directly" refer to any technological aspect of Paradise, since people of different ages, including ourselves, may not know of those technologies. On the other hand, we have been given to understand that we will be rewarded with anything we want: "There will be there all that your souls could desire, all that your eyes could delight in: and you shall abide therein forever." (Az-Zukhruf, 71) In another verse, it is stated that Paradise offers more than we want:

> "There will be for them therein all that they wish,- and more besides in Our Presence." (Qaf, 35) Therefore, everything including technology as well will be available in Paradise, as long as the inhabitants of Paradise so wish it.

The chapter of Ar-Rahman describes Paradise as below;

> "But for such as fear the time when they will stand before the Judgment Seat of their Lord, there will be two Gardens. Containing all kinds (of trees and delights)

> Then which of the favours of your Lord will you deny?

> In each there will be a springs flowing freely. Then which of the favours of your Lord will you deny?

> In them will be fruits of every kind, in paris. Then which of the favours of your Lord will you deny?

They will recline on carpets, whose inner linings will be of rich brocade: the fruit of the Gardens will be near and easy of reach. Then which of the favours of your Lord will you deny?

In them will be maidens, chaste, restraining their glances, whom no man or Jinn before them has touched. Then which of the favours of your Lord will you deny?

Maidens as fair as rubies and coral. Then which of the favours of your Lord will you deny?

Is there any reward for good - other than good? Then which of the favours of your Lord will you deny?

And besides these two, there are two other Gardens, dark-green in colour (from plentiful watering).

A gushing fountain shall flow in each. Then which of the favours of your Lord will you deny?

In them will be fruits, and dates and pomegranates. Then which of the favours of your Lord will you deny?

In them will be fair Companions, good, and beautiful. Then which of the favours of your Lord will you deny?

Companions restrained as to their glances, in (goodly) pavilions. Whom no man or Jinn before them has touched. Then which of the favours of your Lord will you deny?

They shall recline on green cushions and rich, beautiful carpets. Then which of the favours of your Lord will you deny?

Blessed be the name of you Lord, full of Majesty, Bounty and Honour." (Ar-Rahman, 46-78)

Other verses : Paradise is described in a number of;

"And when you gaze upon that scene, you will behold a kingdom which is blissful and magnificent." (Al-Insan, 20)

"Reclining in the Garden on raised thrones, they will feel neither the sun's excessive heat nor the moon's excessive cold." (Al-Insan, 13)

"There they shall hear no word of vanity" (Al-Ghashiya, 11)

"And beside them will be chaste women, restraining their glances, with big eyes (of wonder and beauty), as if they were (delicate) eggs closely guarded." (As-Saffat, 48-49)

"And they will say: 'Praise be to Allah, Who has removed from us (all) sorrow: for our Lord is indeed Oft-Forgiving and Ready to appreciate service: Who has, out of His Bounty, settled us in a Home that will last: no toil nor sense of weariness shall touch us therein.'" (Al-Fatr, 34, 35)

"But it is for those who fear their Lord, that lofty mansions, one above another, have been built: beneath them flow rivers of delight: such is the Promise of Allah: never does Allah fail in His promise." (Az-Zumar, 20)

Allah welcomes his servants as below:

"(To the righteous soul it will be said:) 'O serene soul' Come back to your Lord, joyful yourself and pleasing to Him! Enter, then, among My devotees! Yes, enter My Heaven!'" (Al-Fajr, 27-30)

HELL-MADE READY
FOR THE UNBELIEVERS

∾

Leave to Me the creature whom I created bare and alone!

To whom I granted resources in abundance, and sons to be by his side!

To whom I made life smooth and comfortable! Yet is he greedy

that I should add yet more.

By no means! For to Our Signs he has been refractory! Soon I will visit him mounting calamities! For he thought and he plotted;

Woe to him! How he plotted.

Yes, woe to him! How he plotted!

Then he looked round;

Then he frowned and he scowled;

Then he turned back and was haughty;

Then said he: "This is nothing but magic, derived from of old.

This is nothing but the word of a mortal!"

Soon I will cast him into Hell-Fire!

And what will explain to you what Hell-Fire is? Permit nothing to endure, and leaves nothing alone!

It burns the skin of man. (Al-Muddaththir, 11-29)

For as many beauties and blessings as there are in Paradise, there is an equal amount of ugliness and torment in Hell. Those who have denied Allah as their Creator are punished endlessly in Hell. The following verses of the Qur'an tell us about those who deserve Hell:

"If anyone contends with the Messenger even after guidance has been plainly conveyed to him, and follows a path other than that becoming to men of Faith, We shall leave him in the path he has chosen, and consign him to Hell: an evil refuge." (An-Nisa, 115)

Avoid those who take their religion to be mere play and amusement, and are deceived by the life of this world. But proclaim to them this truth: that every soul delivers itself to ruin by its own acts: it will find for itself no protector or intercessor except Allah: it may offer every ransom, (or reparation), but none will be accepted: such is the end of those who deliver themselves to ruin by their own acts: they shall have only boiling water to drink and shall be sternly punished: for they persisted in rejecting Allah." (Al-Anaam, 70)

"And there are those who bury gold and silver and do not spend it in the way of Allah: announce to them a most grievous penalty. The Day will come when heat will be produced out of that wealth in the fire of Hell, and their foreheads, their flanks, and their backs, will be branded with it. They will be told: This is the treasure which you buried for yourselves: taste you then, the treasures you buried'" (Al-Tawba, 34-35)

"When it is said to them, 'Fear Allah', they are led by arrogance to more crime. Hell shall be enough for them, an evil bed indeed to lie on!" (Al-Baqara, 206)

The common characteristic of unbelievers who deserve to be cast into Hell is their rejection of religion when they have been invited to accept it:

"The Trumpet will be sounded, and all who are in the heavens and on the earth will swoon, except such as it will please Allah to exempt. Then a second trumpet will be sounded, when, behold, they will rise and look around them!

And the Earth will shine with the Glory of its Lord: the Record of Deeds will be laid open; the prophets and the witnesses will be brought forward and all shall be judged with fairness; and they will not be wronged in the least.

And every soul will be paid back in full according to its Deeds; and Allah knows best all that they do.

The Unbelievers will be led to Hell in hordes. When they arrive there its gates will be opened. And its keepers will say, 'Did not messengers come to you from among yourselves, proclaiming to you the revelations of your Lord, and fore warning you of the Meeting of this Day? The answer will be: 'True' And

thus the promised scourge will smite the unbelievers!
They will be told: 'Enter you the gates of Hell, to dwell
therein forever: and evil is this Abode of the
Arrogant!'" (Az-Zumar, 68-72)

According to the Qur'an, the denizens of Hell did not take the penalty of Allah seriously while they were still in this World. At that time they thought that if there were a Hell to which they were to be sent, they would stay there for only a limited period of time. And then, they would be released and would enter Paradise. This is a prevalent view among the members of the society of ignorance. They believe if they are ever to be punished for their sins, they will stay in Hell only, temporarily, and after they have paid for their misdeeds in the world, they will be allowed to enter Paradise. However, the Qur'an informs us that the penalty in Hell will be endless and that there will be no hope of the unbelievers ever entering Paradise.

"And they say: 'The Fire shall not touch us, except
for a few but for a few days,' Say: 'Have you taken
a promise from Allah, for He never breaks His
promise? Or do you assert about Allah what you do
not know?'" (Al Baqara, 80)

"Do but consider those who have been given a portion
of the Book? They are invited to accept the Book of
Allah, to settle their disputes, but some of them turn
back and decline the arbitration. This is because they
say: 'The Fire shall not touch us except for a few days;
In their religion they are deceived by their own lies.
But how will they fare when We gather them together
upon a day about which there is no doubt, and each
soul will be given just what it has earned, without
favour or injustice?" (Al Imran, 23-25)

Other verses of the Qur'an explain the horror in Hell as follows:

"Friends will meet, but shall not speak to each other.
To redeem himself from the Penalty of that Day, the

sinner will gladly sacrifice his children

His wife and his brother,

His kindred who sheltered him,

And all the people on earth, - if that could deliver him:

By no means! For the Fire of Hell

Shall pluck out his being right from the skull!

It shall claim all those who turn their backs and turn away their faces from the Right,

And collect wealth and hide it covetously!" (Al-Maarij, 10-18)

"They shall groan with anguish and be bereft of heaving," (Al-Anbiya, 100)

"In front of such a one is Hell, and he is given, for drink, boiling fetid water.

In gulps he will sip it, but never will he be near swallowing it: death will come to him from every quarter, yet will he not die. Harrowing torment awaits him." (Ibrahim, 16-17)

"And you will see the sinners or that day bound together in fetters;

Their garments of liquid pitch, and their faces covered with Fire." (Ibrahim, 49-50)

Truly, the tree of Zaqqum

Will be the food of the sinful,

Like molten brass; it will boil in their insides,

Like the boiling of scalding water.

A voice will cry: "Seize him and drag him into the midst of the Blazing Fire!

Then pour over his head the Penalty of Boiling Water,

'Taste this! Truly you were mighty and full of honour!'" (Ad-Dukhan, 43-49)

All those descriptions devised for Paradise and Hell are absolute facts. Allah, who has created the world and the life in this world, has revealed the Qur'an and has let us know that He will also create the afterlife.

The question asked of the people of Hell will be: "Did not messengers come to you from among yourselves, reciting to you the revelations of your Lord, and warning you of the Meeting of this Day?" (Az-Zumar, 71)

And for those who have rejected the invitation, there will be a "grievous penalty":

"So he gave nothing in charity, nor did he pray!

But on the contrary, he rejected Truth and turned away!

And then went off to his family, swaggering.

Well have you deserved this doom

Well have you deserved it." (Al-Qiyama, 31-35)

PART TWO

A NEW DIMENSION

∞

At the beginning of this book, we mentioned the instillation in us by society of preconceied ideas. We emphasized that because of such conditioning, we unquestioningly accept many claims, which, in fact, need careful scrutiny. It was also stated that, in order to make a right decision, we need to review our prejudgments, regardless of the subject we are dealing with.

Here in this chapter, we will be questioning one of the most important preconceptions of the current system. We will be bringing to our agenda a subject that has hardly been thought of until now is an attempt to understand the true nature of the 'outer world'. What is the "outer world" which surrounds us really all about?

The source of all the information we have about the 'outer world' is our five senses. Because we have been dependent on our senses from our birth up until now, we do not think the 'outer world' can somehow be different from the picture built up for us by our senses. We are so conditioned to believing that the universe is as we perceive it to be, that we find it unnecessary to discuss this subject

However, recent researches carried out in the scientific arena have led to serious doubts about our perceptions, and the nature of the world perceived through our senses. These researches have pulled down the classical explanations of the universe and matter, and brought a very different dimension and approach to the scientific world, which we call 'a new dimension'

THE WORLD MADE
UP OF ELECTRIC SIGNALS
ॐ

Whatever we perceive as the 'outer world', is in fact a series
of electric signals. Let's take "vision" as an example. The
answer to the question "How do we see?" is usually "With our
eyes, of course." However, the answer is not as simple as this.

Photons entering the eyes pass through a series of
processes. They are converted to electric signals and in this form
are conveyed to the brain. That is, what's conveyed to the brain,
is not photons coming from a perceived object, but electric
signals produced as a reaction to the impact of photons on a
layer of the vision organs called the eyes. In other words, the
vision centre located in the brain does not process the original
light rays but electrical copies of them. When we say, "I am
seeing this object", we don't actually see that object. What we
actually see are electrical signals representing that object in our
brains. We see everything, including the entire universe, in our
vision centre which measures only a couple of square inches.

If we need to interpret the knowledge we have so far, we
can say that the ultimate seeing does not take place in the eyes
but in the vision centre. That is, contrary to common knowledge,
we do not see with our eyes but with the vision centre. Since
no light enters the brain, the brain is always dark. If we verse

to place a photocell, a device that measures light, in your vision centre, we should measure zero light at all times, even while you were directly looking at the sun. To sum up, the brain never sees the object itself but the electric signals that the object gives off. Bertrand Russell gives the following example:

> *"Common sense imagines that when it sees a table it sees a table. This is a gross delusion. When common sense sees a table, certain light-waves reach its eyes, and these are of a sort which, in its previous experience, has been associated with certain sensations of touch, as well as with other people's testimony that they also saw the table. But none of this ever brought us to the table itself. The light-waves caused occurrences in our eyes, and these caused occurrences in the brain. Any one of these, happening without the usual preliminaries, would have caused us to have the sensations we call 'seeing the table', even if there had been no table." (Bertrand Russell, The ABC of Relativity, George Allen and Unwin Ltd., 1958, p. 129)*

This fact related to vision is applicable to all other senses. We smell electric signals, we hear electric signals, and again we taste not the things we eat, but the electric signals representing them.

> *The same is true of the sense of touch. "Even when you run your head against a stone wall, you do not really touch it. When you think you touch a thing, there are certain electrons and protons, forming part of your body, which are attracted and repelled by certain electrons and protons in the thing you think you are touching, but there is no actual contact. The electrons and protons in your body, becoming agitated by nearness to the other electrons and protons, are disturbed, and transmit a disturbance along your nerves to the brain; the effect in the brain is what is necessary to your sensation of contact." (Bertrand*

Russell, In Praise of Idleness and Other Essays, George Allen and Unwin Ltd., 1958, p. 228)

Hearing is no different. Sound waves reaching the ears are converted by the nervous system into electric signals and sent to the hearing centre. As like in the case of the seeing mechanism, it is electrical copies of the sound waves which reach the brain.

THE WORLD AS A FORMATION IN THE BRAIN

ॐ

So far, it has been clearly stated that the objects we see, touch, and hear are simple electric signals which are produced in and interpreted by our brains. When a person eats an apple, for example, several electric impulses are produced and interpreted in his brain. What is perceived as an apple, is not an actual apple but some electrical signals representing its shape, smell, taste and hardness in the brain. In this respect, the outer world introduced to us through our sense organs, is a sum of electrical copies. Our brains, all through our lives, process and evaluate these copies. We believe we are related to "actual" objects, however, we only deal with copies of images.

NO WAY TO THE "ACTUAL" OUTSIDE WORLD

∾

We cannot reach "actual" objects through the senses. So, we can never be sure whether the world formed in our minds is an exact reflection of the actual world. The images formed in our brain may not be similar to actual objects of the outer world. The brain converts the incoming messages into another language within its system and forms a separate universe. As we have been dependent on this system since our birth, we have had no chance to make sure if the brain reflects upon us the actual world and gives the correct information about it. We say "Yes, I'm convinced that it does, because when I perceive a thing, I am told by others that they also perceive the same thing.". Here, however, we forget the fact that those others are also a part of the outside world and therefore a product of our perception. This situation is similar to that of a person who has lived all his life in a room and communicated with the outside world through a screen. It is impossible for this person to assess if the images he watches as the "outside world" really reflect the actual world or not.

To summarize, the way we perceive the "outside world" is based solely on our perception and the interpretation unique to our brain.

> *"In reality, in the universe there exists no light as seen and defined, no sound as heard and no heat as perceived. In other words, our sensory organs deceive us while establishing the relation between the outside world and the brain."* (Prof. Dr. Ali Demirsoy, *Evrenin Çocuklari Children of the Universe, p.3-4)*

Bertrand Russell explains the difference between the "outside world" and the one formed in our brains with the example of a blind man in his book, Philosophical Matters. You can always tell a blind man that light is a wavy movement, something he can conceive of, as visually impaired people orient themselves by touching. Yet, what the blind man understands about light from this definition is totally different from what it really is. Light can never be defined or explained to a blind person. The light described as a wavy movement is totally different from the light we perceive. Therefore, it is impossible to say that the source of the image created in the brain is light. What we are trying to say is that what we see, does not necessarily convey the matter we see in the "outside world". The same phenomenon is also true of the other senses. Let's take another example:

> *"Even the most beautiful symphony is a composition of sound waves that vibrate in our inner ear. All sensations are supposed to be triggered by the outer world. Yet they do not emanate from there but exist as our unique perceptions"* (Bilim ve Teknik (Science and Technique), August, 1988)

In fact, what turns these sound waves in the "outer world" into a symphony is our brain. This means that music does not really occur in the outer world but is only sensed inside us by our brain.

We can arrive at the same result for the perception of colour; while observing different colours, actually different wavelengths of light reach our eyes. It is again our brain that turns these wavelengths into colours. For example, the reason we see an apple as red is the perception of the wavelength of light reflected from the apple to the brain. This means that the apple is not actually red, the sky is not blue and tree is not green; they look that way because of our perception.

> The famous science magazine, "La Recherche", has this to say on this subject: "There is nothing that we can name as red or blue in the light. Physically, we cannot speak of the existence of colour. This is only a psychological perception." (January, 1981)

ANIMALS SEE DIFFERENTLY

∾

Moreover, it is known that animals see objects in different colours and patterns. This is another example that proves that sight is dependent on the perceiver.

For horses, the sky is not blue, but gray. Bees, unlike human beings, are able to perceive ultraviolet colours, so that they see many additional hues. For crocodiles and mice, everything is black and white. Cows and bulls live in a world where the colour red is not known. It is also known that animals observe the shapes of objects differently.

In this case, the question: "Which one is right?" Comes to mind. It is obvious we have no basis for saying that only people see things in the right way.

LIVING IN THE UNIVERSE FORMED BY OUR BRAIN

૱

What makes us say that an object exists is our seeing, touching, or hearing this object. Yet, these sensations do not belong to the object itself, because these are qualities attributed to the object by our brains, or rather, by our minds. This means that those sensations coming from one of the five natural senses like the feeling of heat or pain, are not a part of the "outside world", but all happen inside our minds where they are created.

So, because the "outside world" we are talking about is only a collection of these senses, this outside world cannot exist without a mind. If we abolish all the properties of a fruit, like its sight, smell or taste, the fruit will no longer have a meaning for us. A fruit with no taste, smell, hardness or colour will no longer be called a fruit.

The world we know is actually a world inside our minds where it is designed, given voice and colour or actually created. The only world we are sure of is this one.

To summarize, we live in this world inside our heads where we cannot go a single step further and we are mistaken in thinking that this is the real "outside world". This is not a different interpretation of a philosophy; this is the clear evidence of science.

DOES AN "OUTSIDE WORLD" REALLY EXIST?

∾

The uncertainty originating in the development of science does not focus solely on the qualities of the "outside world". While the new scientific discoveries make us doubt our belief in what we sense, it also brings to mind a dramatic question: "Does an "outside world" really exist?

Have you ever thought about what makes you believe in this "outside world"? Your seeing, hearing or touching of an object is usually enough for you to believe in its existence. However, this is only a belief that you have acquired out of habit possessed with habits, which is contrary to science and logic.

> "As to the sense of touch when we press the table with our fingers, that is an electric disturbance on the electrons and protons of our fingertips, produced, according to modern physics, by the proximity of the electrons and protons in the table. If the same disturbance in our finger-tips arose in any other way, we should have the sensations, in spite of there being no table." (Bertrand Russell, The ABC of Relativity, George Allen and Unwin Ltd., 1958, p. 129-130)

What we want to explain here is that a person can have the sensations of sight, touch or sound, when an object does not even exist. Our brains can form a world as real and lively as the real one with the artificial stimulus it receives.

You may imagine a complex recorder in which many different electric signals are encoded. First, let us record in this recorder all the details of an environment, like its sight, smell, sound and also our own bodies. Then let us forward these electric signals to the relevant parts of the brain. Because all senses like sight, touch and so on are actually triggerd by electric signals in the brain, which are stimulated by this "outside world", we would be deluded into thinking that we were actually in this environment after starting the video system.

In brain surgery, patients see different sights of their friends or scenes when the centre of sight memory is touched. They experience different tastes and start laughing loudly when other corresponding parts of the brain are touched. Therefore, we do not need a real world outside to have a world in our brains; we need only real or artificial stimuli;

DREAMS: THE WORLD
IN OUR BRAINS

Another striking example of the fake world created by the brain is our dreams.

The life we live in our dreams is often extremely "real". A person dreaming that a stranger is following him sweats as he runs across the streets. He becomes so tense that he may even have a heart attack. While all these processes take place, there exists no actual stranger and not even his own body.

In brief, a dream is a clear example of virtual reality where one assumes existence in an actual environment.

What if you are in a dream right now? This may seem an odd question to ask. But just for a minute assume that somebody tells you that what you are experiencing right now is just a dream and all the things happening around you are occurring only in your brain. What would your answer be? It occurs to you that there is no evidence indicating that you are dreaming. Everything seems to be clear, logical and real. There is nothing that will make you suspect otherwise. Consequently, you are not in a dream, But, does the way by which you assess the difference between dreams and reality rest on these criteria? Or is it because the images are so real and seem to be part of a sequence of events?

Beware! The method you used to differentiate dreams from reality does not seem to be scientific. When you are dreaming, you cannot understand whether you are in a dream or not. So, there is no reason to look with contempt at dreams. You talk with somebody that does not exist in reality and want to possess a virtual car. When you wake up, both dreams and the "life" you assume to be real, have the same features and characteristics, since both are experienced in your brain.

When you are dreaming, events develop beyond your control. You are not given the opportunity to choose the place, time and scenario of your dream. Suddenly, you find yourself having an adventure while still asleep. What is more, you do not find the happenings around you strange, although they do not comply with common sense and are against the laws of nature.

Most probably, for you, reality is represented by the things that can be touched and seen. You also hold something with your hand and see it in your dream, where you neither have a hand nor eyes, nor an object to see. This situation is practically deceiving! A philosopher who ponders on this conflict states the following:

> "For while we dream, we do not know that we are dreaming; it is only later, after awaking, that we recognize our dream as a dream. How can we claim that our present experiences are of a more reliable type than those of a dream? The fact that they are associated with a feeling of reality does not make them more dependable, because we have the same feeling in a dream. We cannot completely exclude the possibility that later experiences will prove that we are dreaming even now." (Hans Reichenbach, The Rise of Scientific Philosophy, University of California Press, 1973, p.29)

> Descartes also made the same proposition: "In my dreams I see myself going to places; when I wake up I realize that I have been nowhere and I find myself

*just lying in my bed. Who can assure me that I am
not dreaming right now, or that my whole life is not
a dream? For these reasons, the reality of the world
I live in becomes a totally dubious concept." (Macit
Gökberk, Felsefe Tarihi (History of Philosophy),
p.263)*

Then what is the difference between real life and dreams?
Is it the fact that real life has an uninterrupted, continuous
nature, or is it because a different kind of reasoning mechanism
prevails in dreams? These are not important differences in
principle, since both kinds of life experience occur in the brain.

If we can live in a virtual life when dreaming, why
wouldn't we be living in a virtual life when we are not
dreaming? There is no logical reason to prevent us from
thinking that we are starting to live in a longer dream that we
call "real life", when we wake up from a dream. It is our
prejudice and traditional way of thinking which lead us to have
no doubts about this subject, although we do not have any solid
evidence about it.

THE WORLD FORMED BY HYPNOSIS

Under hypnosis, the patient although in a deep sleep hears, sees and feels as instructed by another person. The hypnotist can verbally simulate any environment and the patient would believe that he is in that environment and that the environment is real. In General Hospital Psychiatry magazine (January 1987), an experiment performed on a ten-year-old boy whose leg had been broken in a car accident is related as follows:

> "The patient was requested to close his eyes and feel as if he were in a cinema. During the operation, the boy lay calmly and moved his right hand regularly between his mouth and his knee. In the meantime, the doctor took care of the fracture. What were the rhythmic hand movements? After he woke up, the boy said that he had been eating popcorn in the cinema."

Under hypnosis, you can make somebody hear the voices you choose. If we convince him that our voice comes out of a wall, he will think that the wall speaks. If we go further and say that the voice comes from our hands or ears, he will assume that these organs talk.

Moreover, the time concept in hypnosis is also quite different. An experiment carried out in Virginia University Psychology Department is worth mentioning. A university student was hypnotized and told to return to her high school years and go into each classroom in her school. There were around 20 classrooms in her school and she was instructed to tell what was happening in each classroom one by one. Yet, she had only half an hour to accomplish this and a metronome was regulating the time. The girl was told that a metronome would tick each minute, so that she would know how much time was left for her to finish.

The hypnotized girl managed her time well and accomplished what was expected of her in the time given. Yet the metronome was ticking not every minute, but every second. In other words, the metronome functioned for a total of 30 seconds, not half an hour.

After 30 seconds, the metronome was stopped and the professor woke the girl up. Then he asked what she remembered of the experience Her subconscious had worked according to the way it was instructed, and so she was able to recount in detail what she saw in each room. When she learned that the whole experiment had lasted for 30 seconds and not half an hour, she was very astonished.

This example shows how an illusionary world can certainly be created through hypnosis. So much so that even if we kept only the brain of a human being alive, we could give him a body and a face at will through hypnosis, and we could make him live a life just like the one we are living right now.

HOLOGRAM: THREE DIMENSIONAL DREAM

∾

Apart from the human brain's ability to make up virtual locations, modern technology supplies us with the tools to establish three-dimensional "virtual worlds". The three-dimensional technique of photography, the product of which is called a "hologram", is generated with the help of laser rays.

The images produced by a hologram rest in space and it is possible to see the image from all angles. Today, the hologram is commonly used in daily life activities, like exhibiting precious jewelry or presenting theater decorations. As long as it is not touched, it is impossible to differentiate a hologram from its original.

All these examples indicate a certain fact; "The brain cannot distinguish whether the stimulus comes from a real or a fake source."

In other words, the fact that we see, touch or smell a susbstance does not mean that it actually exists. While dreaming, under hypnosis, or when our nerves are artificially stimulated, we have no doubts about the reality of the setting we are in. However, the setting which we assume to be real, occurs only the brain.

In short, our brain or, in more accurate terms, our mind

presents a world to us. It is impossible for us to acquire any idea about the real nature of the existence of this world.

Then, how can we be sure about the existence of this world that we live in and assume it to be real? Although there is no scientific and logical support for the existence of a real world, the reason why we believe in it rests in traditional ways of thinking and the way we have been gathering our knowledge and perceptions of the world since the time we were born. We can clearly see this fact when we set our mind free and think without the limitations of our prejudices.

THE REAL NATURE OF MATTER

ᐒ

From medicine to physics and in many other branches of science, recent developments have revealed serious doubts about the reality of the "outside world". Scientists and astronomers state that the real nature of the universe is not matter, but they also add that perfect order prevails. For instance, Einstein says: "I feel astonished when I see the order of the universe." Astronomer Arthur Eddington, on the other hand, expresses the view that the basic cement of the universe is thought. James Jeans, another astronomer, also agrees with the above viewpoints and states that the universe is like a great thought rather than a big machine.

The recent developments that have taken place in science over the last century have made certain theories regarding the nature of the world and the actual existence of matter collapse and replaced them with a brand new concept.

One of the most important studies pertaining to the real nature of matter is Einstein's relativity theory. Einstein, with his famous formula $E=mc^2$, asserted that matter is a form of energy. In other words, the basic unit of matter is energy, which does not take up any space and does not have any volume and mass. In this case, it is impossible to state that matter has volume or mass, and that it has an existence in the sense in which we perceive it.

> "Before the relativity theory, scientists accepted the existence of two separate concepts in the universe as matter and energy. Matter was thought to have volume and mass and energy was defined as a wavy, invisible concept that lacked a mass. Albert Einstein revealed that these two concepts are the same and proved that what is perceived as matter is, in essence, energy. In other words, matter is energy and energy is matter." (Ali Demirsoy, Evren ve Çocuklari (Universe and Its Children), p.18)

Another development that rendered void the classical definitions of matter is that of quantum physics. During atomic research, it has been observed that a deeper analysis of atoms indicated a different nature of the atom. That is because the quarks, the basic part of the atom, are not matter but energy. These particles can not be defined as matter since they lack volume and mass and do not take up any space. For instance, photons are also quarks. In this case the atom which is made up of these particles cannot be defined as matter. To conclude, since the basic element of the "outside world" is the atom, it is not possible to talk about the actual existence of the universe. To say it in another way, the universe is made up of atoms, which cannot be called matter.

> "All kind of matter in the universe, whether in the form of gas or liquid, are formed of various waves. We live in an ocean of waves and perceive different levels of energy in the form of different senses." (Ali Demirsoy, Evren ve Çocuklari (Universe and Its Children), p.6)

Aydin Aritan, a writer of Bilim ve Teknik (Science and Technique) magazine states the following:

> "The universe is also made up of waves, of various vibrations having different frequencies. Quantum

physics tells us that these vibrations compose the dimensions and the matter we perceive. Yet we do not perceive the "outside world" as waves but as pictures and forms of matters. In this case, the outside world and all its perceptions are just a misperception, just as Berkeley said once upon a time."

"According to Einstein's theory of relativity, the world appears not as a structure built out of independently existing, unanalyzable entities, but rather as a web of relationships among elements whose meanings arise entirely from their relationship to the whole. Similarly, quantum mechanics can lead to the views that physical reality is essentially nonsubstantial - that fields or relationships alone are real. The eastern mystics knew that. They called the separation of objects maya, an illusion which comes from our categorizing intellect." (Newsweek, August 13, 1979, p. 46)

As it is seen, the "outside world" as it is commonly referred to, is nothing but an ocean of waves that has neither mass, nor volume, nor location. Then why do we perceive it as regular images? The answer is we live in a world generated by the mind. Colour, voice, mass, strength, shape and other features are all concepts generated by the mind and have no actual existence in the "outside world".

Aydin Aritan outlines this concept as follows: "We perceive the outside world as forms of matter and pictures, because our brain and senses are organized in this way. Yet this does not mean that the outside world has these features in reality."

"If we try to know the universe through our senses we cannot find the truth. If we try to know it through means other than our senses, then we come across with spirit lacking mathematical formulas." (Ali Demirsoy, Evren ve Çocuklari (Universe and Its Children), p.7)

Neurologist Karl Pilgram, who is known for his research on the actual existence of the "outside world", states that the "outside world" is just a hologram composed of waves decoded by the brain:

> "In a symposium held in Minnesota, Pilgram stated that the answer might be in Gestalt psychology. In other words, the perceived substance acquires a reality with the type of perception the perceiver has. Maybe the whole world is nothing but a hologram. Is the audience sitting across from him a hologram? Are they frequencies decoded by his own brain and the brains of others? If the nature of reality is holographic matter, then the world, just as depicted in the Far East philosophies, is just a misperception." (Güneş (The Sun), September 9 ,1990)

Finally, when we free our minds from prejudice, we can see that there is no solid evidence proving the existence of a real world.

At this stage, the following question is the first one that comes to mind: "If there is not an outside world, what is the source of the images we see around us? How do we feel that we live in a real and actual world?"

Before answering these questions, let us have a look at the recent technological developments that will assist us to comprehend the subject better.

SIMULATOR;
ARTIFICIAL REALITY

∾

The technique called **"simulation"** generates an artificial virtual world with the help of a computer. A helmet with a screen provides you with a three-dimensional image and makes the brain believe that it is experiencing the real world by exciting the five senses attached to it. A computer that is equipped with the latest techniques of simulation and modeling that can almost handle all five of our human senses, provides the excitement to the brain. How is this done? And what are its implications?

It is done, essentially, by applying advanced forms of imaging with which we are already familiar from 3D virtual reality games. In order to train F16 pilots, LCD masks or helmets have been designed that show the pilot a three dimensional picture of the aircraft such that, as he moves his head up and down, it feels to him as if he were really in the aircraft. With the addition of a perfect sound system and a seat that moves in sensitive accord with what is represented through the LCD helmet, all the thrills and sensations of flying can be "experienced" by the trainee pilot.

This example shows the fact that sensory effects can easily produce a virtual world.

WHO IS THE ONE THAT SEES?

∾

"Is the "outside world" really there, or are we producing it in our brain? It is an established fact that we have five senses. It is also obvious that senses reach the brain through the nervous system and brain stores this processed data. Yet, what or who lives data actually, and organizes the sensory stimulus and converts it in a conscious mechanism that is referred to as the perception of the "outside world"?" (Gelisim Bilim ve Teknik Ansiklopedisi (Encyclopedia Gelisim of Science and Technique), p.1216)

There is no doubt that the world we live in is formed in the brain. However, the main question arises at this point. If all the things that we see and live through do not have a materialistic existence like dreams-how are these images generated?

It is sometimes said that these images are a "function of the brain that has not yet been yet solved". In this case, the dream is produced by the memory in an unknown way. In fact, when the question: Who shows these images in the brain?" is asked, it is said, though without any evidence that the "brain itself" generates them.

WHO IS THE ONE THAT SEES? 113

At this point, we must take up another aspect of the issue which we have disregarded up to now. Bertrand Russell states;

> "Of course, if matter in general is to be interpreted as a group of occurrences, this must apply also to the eye, the optic nerve and the brain" (Bertrand Russell, The ABC of Relativity, George Allen and Unwin Ltd., 1958, p. 129)

In other words, the brain is also a part of the "outside world" which is now comprehended to be nothing but a collection of images having no location, mass or volume. An example about a dream will make our point clear. Now, let us assume that we are having a dream in our brain. In our dream: we will have a virtual body, and hence virtual eyes and brain. If somebody asks in our dream: Where do we see the world?", our answer would be "in my brain". If the same person goes further and asks where is our brain and what it looks like, then we would grab our virtual head and say "my brain is in my skull weighing almost a kilogram."

It is evident that there is no brain but a virtual head and a virtual brain in our dream. The one that sees the images is not the virtual brain in the dream but an existence "beyond" it.

Actually, there is no observable difference between the setting of the dream and of the "real world" as we call it. Therefore, when we come pose the same question in our daily life, giving the same type of answer would not make much sense. The one that sees is "beyond" the brain, and it is an existence marked by totally different characteristics.

This "existence" is something that feels, touches, sees, hears, loves, fears and refers to itself as "I". This "existence" is a "living organism", yet it is neither matter nor an image. It is also nonsense to call it a body part weighing 1 kilo and 300 grams. That is because, it is impossible for the atoms that make up the cells to create a perfect three-dimensional world. When a deep analysis of the brain is made, we come across natural structures such as amino acids, molecules that are common in every part of the universe. In other words, in the brain there exists no location or structure that generates the images or makes up the consciousness.

Obviously the "existence" that feels, sees, thinks and calls itself "I", is somewhere beyond the brain. Religion refers to this existence as the "spirit". The "outside world", on the other hand, just as in our dream, takes the form of the images presented to our spirit by Allah. In other words, the human being is not in the universe but the universe, is in the human being.

The reason why the "outside world" seems to be so realistic is the perfection of the senses and the images. Our Creator creates a perfect world for us. What misleads us is the excellence of the creation of these images. Briefly, we can define the universe, as an image perfect enough to call it almost "real".

How does the Qur'an deal with the issue?

What we have said until now facilitates the comprehension of certain important facts; the real nature of the universe manifests itself in the explanations given above and puts an end to the sovereignty of the materialistic approach, which was valid in the past, in the explanation of the being of Allah and human beings.

The materialistic approach is based on the assumption that matter has an absolute existence. Now that we know matter is not absolute but an entity made up of perceptions and images, the power attributed wrongly to matter should now be seen as belonging to Allah Who creates all of these images. Since matter is collection of perceptions, the concepts of space and location also become nonsense.

In this case, the answer to the classical question: "Where is Allah?" becomes clear. According to those who do not adhere to the Qur'anic way of life and thinking, Allah is "up in the sky" watching them from a distance and rarely interfering with worldly affairs. This mentality separates the universe that is made up of matter from Allah. The understanding of Allah is some religions is based on this mentality. same mentality also prevails in the societies of ignorance whose members claim to be Muslims.

Yet, as it has been emphasized until now, matter is just a perception. It is not an alternative for Allah to exist outside this collection of matter. Allah is everywhere. Nothing can be out of Allah's existence.

A number of verses in the Qur'an make this explanation more accurate.

> "Behold! We told you that your Lord encompasses mankind." (Al-Isra, 60)

> "But to Allah belong all things in the heavens and on earth: And He it is that Encompasses all things." (An-Nisa, 126)

> "Ah indeed! It is He that encompasses all things!" (Fussilat, 54)

> "To Allah belong the east and the west: wherever you turn, there is the presence of Allah. For Allah is all-Pervading, all-Knowing." (Al-Baqara, 115)

> "And He is Allah in the heavens and on earth." (Al-Anaam, 3)

> "He to whom belongs the dominion of the heavens and the earth: no son has He begotten, nor has He a partner in His dominion: it is He who created all things, and ordered them in due proportion." (Al-Furqan, 2)

> "...for We are nearer to him than (his) jugular vein." (Qaf, 16)

> "Allah is He, besides Whom there is no other god-He knows all things both secret and open; He, is the Most Gracious, the Most Merciful. Allah is He,

besides Whom there is no other god-the Sovereign, the Holy One, the Source of Peace and Perfection, the Guardian of Faith, the Preserver of Safety, the Exalted in Might, the Irresistible, the Supreme: Glory to Allah! High is He above the partners they attribute to Him. He is Allah, the Creator, the Evolver, the Bestower of Forms (or Colours). His are the Most Beautiful Names: whatever is in the heavens and on earth, declares His Praises and Glory: and He is the Exalted in Might, the Wise one." (Al-Hashr, 22-24)

Islamic intellectuals, who adopted the Qur'anic point of view in their interpretation of the universe realized centuries ago that the universe is not of a materialistic nature, and made very explicit statements about the real nature of the things created by Allah. One of the most prominent thinkers of Islamic history, Imam Rabbani, stated his views as follows:

"Allah chose various objects to reveal each of His epithets (Just, Gracious, Provider of Sustenance) and He reflected His own attributes on these objects. The substance of these beings on which He reflected His epithets is nothingness. The Glorious Allah chose various objects for each of His epithets in the realm of nothingness and created those in the sphere of senses and illusions. And He did so whenever He liked and however He liked.

The existence of the universe in the sphere of senses and illusions, and it is not external. In this circumstance, a constancy emerges in nothingness in the sphere of senses and illusions and it acquires tenacity and strength by the creation of Allah, the Most High. Thus it becomes something that lives, knows, acts, wills, sees, hears and speaks. Through reflection and shadow are its name and sign presented in the outside world. In reality, there is nothing in the outside except the epithets and attributes of Allah.

All these have appeared on the mirror of the evident presence of Allah, the Superior One. There is nothing outside but these appearances. They have thus acquired an image in the outside world. They seemed as though they really existed. In the real sense, there is nothing outside but Allah, the Glorious." (Imam Rabbani, Mektubati Rabbani (Letter of Rabbani), p. 517-519)

The interpretation of another very important Islamic thinker, Said Nursi also conveys the same message:

> "The materialistic world has a virtual nature, being a reflection of Allah's existence. It comes to be a real world by the command of Allah. It becomes consistent and constant by Allah's will. The world of matter is neither a real world, nor a dreamy and temporary shadow. It exists only by the creation of Allah." (Mektubat (The Letters), p.503)

In conclusion, the "outside world", including our body is an image projected to our spirit by Allah. Therefore, it does not have an existence of its own. The universe is inside man and what surrounds man is not matter, but Allah. This fact is thus made explicit: "We know the prompting of his soul, and are closer to him than his jugular vein."

Many verses in the Qur'an describe the different aspects of the structure of creation:

> "Do they indeed ascribe to Him as partners things that can create nothing, but are themselves created?" (Al-Araf, 191)

> "Those whom they invoke besides Allah create nothing and are themselves created." (An-Nahl, 20)

The following verse pertains to the continual creation of Allah and clearly explains how every image is perfectly created by Allah.

> Surely, worthier is He who has made His creatives and will bring them back to life in the hereafter; Who gives you sustenance from earth and sky."…. (Al-Naml, 64)

The continuous existence of the universe depends solely on Allah's will to continue His creation. It is just like a TV program that can be watched only so long as it is broadcast by a TV channel.

Since Allah creates the images, every action is also created by Him. This means that when we walk, run or laugh, all images related to these actions are presented only because Allah so wills it. Some verses of the Qur'an come to mind for their striking relevance to this discussion:

> "It is not you who slew them; it was Allah: when you threw, it was not your act, but Allah's: in order that He might test the Believers by a gracious trial from Himself: for Allah is He Who hears and knows all things." (Al-Anfal, 17)

> "But Allah has created you and your handiwork!" (As-Saaffat, 96)

> "...But, truly, the command is with Allah in all things.." (Al-Rad, 31)

To summarize, everybody is under the control of Allah and no event can be realized except by the will and control of Allah. The fact that Allah projects all images in our minds is not limited to a few verses. Moreover, from the Qur'an we learn that Allah sometimes makes people perceive some events differently.

> "There has already been a Sign for you in the two armies that met in combat: One was fighting in the cause of Allah, the other resisting Allah; the faithfull saw with their own eyes that they were twice their own number. But Allah supports with His aid whom He pleases. In this is a warning for such as have eyes to see." (Al Imran, 13)

SLEEP, DREAMS, DEATH AND THE HEREAFTER

∾

What is stated in the Qur'an about sleep has significance with respect to the above-mentioned subject. In the Qur'an, sleep is described as follows:

> "It is Allah that takes the souls (of men) at death; and those that do not die He takes during their sleep: those on whom He has passed the decree of death, He keeps back (from returning to life), but the rest He sends to their bodies for an appointed term. Truly, in this are Signs for those who reflect." (Az-Zumar, 42)

> "It is He who takes your souls by night, and has knowledge of all that you have done by day: by day. He raises you up again so that an allotted term may be fulfilled. In the end to Him you will all return; then He will show you the truth of all that you did. " (Al-Anaam, 60)

In the Qur'an, the state of sleeping is referred to as "death". No significant discrimination is made between sleep and death. This is a clear indication that what is experienced while sleeping is very similar to what one goes through when one dies.

Well, what is common to sleep and death, and what kind

of significance does it have? In sleep, one's spirit leaves the body, or rather, Allah takes it. In dreaming, on the other hand, the spirit gains a new body and starts to perceive a totally different setting. What is referred to as being "raised up" in the verse is the return of the spirit to the actual body and continuing to experience what is called "daily life".

That is to say, death puts an end to the life we experience in the world, by which process the spirit gains a new body and with it makes a new start to an entirely different life. This is actually a key concept that clarifies some notions about religion that may seem hard to comprehend. For instance, death and resurrection are just an interchange of images presented to our spirit by Allah. Everyday, every moment, Allah recreates the world for us and presents our spirit with a continuous display of beauty. The same thing is also valid for sleep. The delicate images created during the course of a day are created at night in our dreams. Similarly, the transition from this world to the next world may be as smooth as passing to a phase of sleep; the images pertaining to this world turn into the images of the other world and death serves as a transition point.

Dreams are also images perceived by our soul just like those experienced in our daily lives. The verse below first reminds us of Allah's closeness to man and then explains for what purpose Allah creates the dreams.

> "Behold! We told your that your Lord encompasses mt ,ikind: We granted the vision which We showed you, but as a trial for men." (Al-Isra , 60)

Since dreams are presented to the human spirit by Allah, there may be some kind of dreams from which people receive news of impending events. There are many examples of such dreams in the Qur'an, such as (Al Fath, 27) the Prophet Joseph's dreams, which he sees in different phases of his life. Just pondering on dreams will make one understand the foregoing assertions. People who attribute dreams to be a function of the brain, say that during dreaming, they receive certain signals from the brain and that this is evidence showing that everything happens in the brain. Yet, it should not be forgotten that Allah creates everything according to the cause and effect relationship. This means that the body and spirit of human beings are closely interrelated. Emotions like sorrow, trouble, love, etc. having an effect on the brain is a normal consequence of the relation between body and spirit. Yet, it is not the brain but the spirit that experiences the emotions.

THE RELATIVITY
OF TIME

∾

Time and space have also been created by Allah who is the Creator of everything. Before, there was no space and time. Actually, there was even no "before", as this refers to a period of time according to the current physical rules that are limited to space and time. However looked at, time and space are only perceptions. Various verses of the Qur'an emphasize time as a relative concept:

> "He will say: 'What number of years did you stay on earth?' They will say: 'We stayed a day or part of a day: just ask those who keep an account.' He will say: "Brief indeed was your sojourn, if you but knew it!" (Al-Mumenoon, 112-114)

> "The Day when the Trumpet will be sounded on that Day, We shall gather the sinful, blear-eyed with terror. In whispers they will consult each other: 'You tarried not longer than ten days': We know best what they will say, when their leader most eminent in conduct will say: 'You tarried not longer than a day!'" (Ta-ha, 102-104)

The verses indicate that in the hereafter, the life we live in the world, which seems to be continuing for years, will be found to have lasted no longer than a moment, just as time passes in dreams and under hypnosis. When we have a dream during sleep, we think that it lasts for hours and days. However, scientific findings show that it lasts only a couple of minutes or even seconds. Similarly, the time in this world will be reckoned to have been very short when we wake up from this lifetime sleep.

MISLEADING CAUSE
AND EFFECT
RELATIONSHIPS
ও

From the time we were born, we have been told to link certain
effects to certain causes. This is actually a natural consequence
of the thinking process of the materialistic mentality. However,
the Qur'an gives information about a different kind of rule
prevailing on earth.

> "Have you not turned your eyes to your Lord? How
> He prolongs the shadow! If He willed, He could make
> it stationary! Then We make the sun its guide." (Al-
> Furqan, 45)

Here in this verse, it is stated that the shadow is created
separately from the Sun, and does not appear as a natural
consequence of it. It is also emphasized that the Sun is provided
as "evidence" for a shadow.

The sun-shadow example in this verse indicates that no
incident occurs as a consequence of a cause, but that both cause
and effect are in reality created by Allah. In other words, the
reason for things happening is not those that seem to cause
them. Power rests with Allah and Allah creates each image
every moment of time. Life has an existence only because Allah

creates it. The verse "Allah is the One who creates you and your actions" clearly expresses this fact.

When we remember that there is no difference between the perception of the outside world and dreams, we have a better understanding about the relation between the shadow and the sun. Is the shadow we see in our dreams cast because of a sun? How is it that a non-existing sun causes a shadow to exist? What is more, sometimes the shining sun we see in our dreams may cause our eyes to be dazzled. In such a dream, since there is no actual sunlight, the feeling of dazzling is specially and separately created. The same logic holds true for perceiving the taste of a fruit that we eat or the pain we feel when we hit an object in our dream.

The reason why we perceive natural events in terms of cause and effect is because of Allah's creation of the sequence of these events. This resembles the frames of a film; our life is formed of these frames created one by one. For example; in the first square there is the tree and in the second one, the fruit. The reason why people think that tree is the cause of the fruit is because of these events occurring one after the other. However, Allah creates both the tree and the fruit separately.

"FUTILE NAMES":
LAWS OF NATURE
∾

In the light of all this information, one should ponder upon what "laws of nature" really are. In a setting where everything is formed of images or senses, how can a "law" originate? Can water have "a lifting force"? Also, how can the friction force of the air be explained, when the air is actually imaginary?

Verses of the Qur'an give clear explanations of these laws of nature, contrary to the generally accepted materialistic view:

> "Do they not look at the birds, held poised in the midst of (the air and) the sky? Nothing holds them up but the power of Allah. Turly, in this are signs for those who believe." (An-Nahl, 79)

> "Your Lord is He That makes the Ship go smoothly for you across the sea, in order that you may seek his Bounty..." (Al-Isra, 66)

> "It is Allah Who causes the seed-grain and the date-stone to split and sprout. He causes the living to issue from the dead, and He is the one to cause the dead to issue from the living. That is Allah: then how can you turn away from the truth?" (Al-Anaam, 95)

The things that we call 'laws of nature' arise from a successive creation pattern of Allah. Allah creates the image of a seed as a cause before creating the image of a flower. The image of the flower is never created before the seed. Although Allah is the Creator of all causes and effects, the created results are always tied up to certain causes.

Eventually, the 'law of nature' is only the name given to this process of successive creation. For example, because ships are always created sailing on water, we talk of the capacity of water to keep things afloat. Similarly 'when we see the birds flying, we say that aerodynamic force is the reason for it. However, the verses in the Qur'an stating that Allah is holding birds in the sky, and making the ships sail for you explain the reality that there is no force other than that of Allah and that all images are created in this way. So, the laws of nature, like water's "lifting force" and gravitation, that we think of as existing, are actually our designation of the sequential and perfect creation we observe.

Einstein describes this reality as follows:

> *"Subjects like gravity, electromagnetic force, energy, electricity and momentum are all theoretical structures, similarities and symbols formed by the human mind in order to explain the basic reality underlying everything we see." (Bilim ve Teknik (Science and Technique), v.272, p.28)*

> *"All power and honour belong to Allah" (Yunus, 65). The power and honour belonging to Allah are called by such names as "gravitation" and "energy". It can be easily understood after a moment of thought that these names actually have no meaning at all.*

To sum up, materialistic people and groups who are keen on making up imaginary deities to believe in, have madeup meaningless terms like "mother nature" — futile words. The Prophet Joseph's words in the Qur'an reflect this fact clearly:

"If not Him, you worship nothing but names which you have devised,- you and your fathers,- for which Allah has sent down no authority: the command is for none but Allah: He has commanded that you worship none but Him: that is the right religion, but most men do not understand. " (Yusuf, 40)

What confuses us is maybe the unawareness of most people of this fact as stated in the verse. However, the individual will understand better that this world is only imagination when he finds himself in the hereafter. Right now, one should start thinking and understanding the existence of Allah. Because, the situation of the unbelievers in the hereafter is described as follows in the Qur'an:

"As for the Unbelievers, their deeds are like a mirage in sandy deserts, which the man parched with thirst mistakes for water; until when he comes up to it, he finds it to be nothing: But he finds Allah (ever) with him, and Allah will pay him his account: and Allah is swift in taking account." (Al-Noor, 39)

PART THREE

MIRACLES JUST BESIDES US

ᜂ

*We did not create the heavens, the earth, and all between them, merely in idle sport: We crea*ed *them to reveal the truth: but most of then. do not understand. (Dukhan, 38-39)*

At the beginning of the book we gave the example of a man who had been "suddenly" created. We described how this person would inspect his own being and his environment with great admiration and amazement. It was also pointed out that our own situation is not a bit different from this man's; however, because of the behaviour and habits acquired from society, we have forgotten how to be amazed, astonished or even affected in any way by the excellence that exists around us. In other words, we have lost our ability to realize the miracles lying right in front of our eyes.

One of the most important subjects covered in the verses of the Qur'an is the need for breaking this indifference that has developed because of these habits and flawed thinking. While some verses of the Qur'an describe people going astray when awaiting miracles or other proof of Allah before they accept Him, other verses refer to a source of reality in miraculous phenomena which are already in existence everywhere.

According to the Qur'an, all living things constitute evidence of the existence and omnipotence of Allah. The reason for this is that every creation of Allah is characteristic of the designation of a Creator. Actually, displaying Allah's precise and gentle work of art and infinite intelligence is the impetus for their creation.

We are now going to reflect on specific examples of animals that are given in the Qur'an.

> *"And in the creation of yourselves and the fact that animals are scattered over the earth, are Signs for those of assured Faith." (Al-Jathiya, 4)*

THE HONEYBEE

Ɔᴗ

"And your Lord taught the Bee"

"And your Lord taught the Bee to build its cells in hills, on trees, and in men's habitations; then to eat of all the produce (of the earth), and find with skill the spacious paths of its Lord: there issues from within their bodies a drink of varying colours, wherein is healing for men: truly in this is a Sign for those who give thought." (Nahl, 68-69)

The above verse of the Qur'an, in the chapter named "An-Nahl" or "honeybee", informs us that this tiny animal has many mysteries of creation within itself. Do you yourself ever remember thinking about the complex story of that delicious food, honey, and its producer, the honeybee?

In fact, bees store this wonderful food named honey in preparation for the winter months when it is going to be hard for them to find flowers. Normally, animals do not trouble to store food exceeding the actual amount they can consume. However, bees produce honey in quantities, several times greater than their actual needs. This is just the same as the hen unne ˸sarily laying eggs daily or the cow producing milk more than its newborn would ever need.

Certainly, the first question that comes to mind is; Why has this "excess production" lasting for tens of thousands of years not terminated? The answer to this question lies in the above verse that explains how the bee is taught to produce honey.

The lives of bees in the hive and their honey production are very interesting in their processes. Without going into too much detail, let us discover more about the primary properties of the bees' "social life".

Regulation of humidity: The temperature in the hive has to be 32 degrees Celsius for 10 months of the year during the brooding period. Humidity, which principally causes honey to attain its protective quality, must be kept within a certain limit in the hive. If this limit is exceeded, the honey is spoiled and loses its protective and nutritious qualities. In order to constantly maintain the temperature and humidity in the hive within these exact limits, a special "ventilation group" is appointed solely for this important task.

Air conditioning: Bees ventilate the hive to make it cool and produce honey with the right humidity level. The same ventilation system is used to safeguard the hive from smoke and air pollution.

During a hot day, it is easy to observe the bees ventilating the hive. They round into the entrance and by clamping on to the wooden floor, they use their wings to fan the hive. In a standard hive, the incoming air is forced to leave from the other side. Extra ventilators in the hive also allow the air to be pushed in four different directions.

Now another question comes to mind, how do the bees "plan" and "carry out" the operations for the regulation of humidity and air conditioning? These operations need immense "intelligence" and "consciousness". We already know that it is not possible for these animals to possess these abilities. Then, the real source of this intelligence and consciousness must be found.

Health system: The efforts of the bees to preserve the quality of the honey are not confined to humidity regulation and air conditioning. A wonderful health system functions in the hive to control all events that may result in the origination of bacteria. This system firstly aims at destroying all places that may possibly result in the production of bacteria. The basic principle of this health system is to prevent foreign objects from entering the hive. Because of this, there are always two guardians at the hive's entrance. If a foreign substance or insect enters the hive despite this prevention, all bees get into action to keep it out of the hive.

For the bigger foreign objects that cannot be carried outside, another prevention mechanism is started. Bees produce a substance called "propolis, or bee resin" for these kinds of situations. They formulate it by gathering resin from trees like pine, poplar and acacia, then combine it with some special secretions. The basic utility of propolis is its resistance to bacterial invasion. Dangerous sorts of substances are therefore, covered with 1.5 mm thick propolis, and isolated from the hive.

Interestingly, this same bee resin is used to patch any cracks in the hive. This resin reacts with the air and forms a hard surface after drying in a very short time. Even though we assume that bees secrete this substance "consciously" to cover foreign particles, etc., how can we explain the bees giving an antibacterial quality to this secretion? Do you, who have a more developed intelligence than the bee, possess the ability to give an antibacterial quality to any of the secretions of your own body?

It is very evident that the system bees implement when protecting the hive again needs great consciousness and intelligence.

Finally, it is abundantly clear that the bee's body and its secretions are precisely "designed" and created.

Cleaning: Bees never leave their feces inside the hive; they excrete when flying or far away from the hive.

Cells: Honeybees shape small beeswax cells and construct a hive in which 30.000 bees live and work together.

The hive is made up of beeswax-walled honeycombs with many tiny cells on their surfaces. All the cells forming the honeycomb have exactly the same dimensions. This engineering

miracle is multiplied by the collective functioning of thousands
of bees. Bees use these cells for food storage and maintenance
of the young bees.

Bees have used the hexagonal structure in the formation
of the honeycomb for millions of years. Why have they chosen
the hexagonal formation rather than octagonal, spherical or
pentagonal structures? Mathematicians have spent a great deal
of effort on finding the answer to this question. Calculations
proved that the hexagonal structure was the most suitable and
convenient geometric form to gain maximum benefit from the
unit area in the honeycomb. If the honeycomb cells were
formed in another structure, then there would be spare places
left out of use; thus less honey would be stored. Also the
population of the bees using the hive would be less. Another
advantage of the hexagonal cell is that while containing the
maximum amount of honey; it needs the minimum amount of
wax for construction.

The honeycomb as an architectural miracle: The
construction of the honeycomb is started from the upper side
of the hive and continued simultaneously in two or three
separate rows downward. While a single honeycomb expands
in two opposite directions, the lower ends of its two rows must
join. This job is realized with remarkable cooperation and
organization. So, it is never possible to tell that the honeycomb
was originally constituted by a process involving three separate
parts. The pieces of honeycomb produced from separate
starting points are combined with such skill that, although
there are hundreds of different angles in its structure, it seems
like one uniform piece.

The cells combining these two rows also have a perfect
hexagonal structure and the same dimensions as all the others.
Not even one cell is different from the others. Scientists are
deeply surprised at how the work of thousands of bees is
marked by such precise calculation.

Determination of direction: Honeybees usually have to fly
long distances and trace out large territories to find food. They
gather flower dust and honey constituents within a range of

800 meters from their hive. The bee, which finds the flowers, flies back to the hive to inform the others about their location. But, how will this bee describe this place to its friends?

The bee returning to the hive starts to perform a kind of a dance. This dance is a way of explaining the location of the flower source to the other bees. This dance, repeated many times by the bee, includes information about the direction, distance and other details to enable the other bees to reach the target. This dance of the bee is actually performed by drawing figure of 8 in the air. The bee forms the middle part of the eight by shaking its tail and making zig-zags. The angle between the zig-zags and the line between the sun-hive, gives the exact direction of the food source.

However, knowing only the direction of the food source is not enough. Worker bees should also possess information regarding the distance of the hive from the source before going there. So, the bee returning from the flower source shakes its body several times to tell the distance. For example, in order to express a distance of 250 m., it shakes the bottom part of its body 5 times in half a minute. In this way, the exact is defined in terms of both distance and angle.

If the journey from the hive to the source is taking a long time, a new problem arises for the bee. The sun moves 1 degree every four minutes. Eventually, while describing the location of the food source, the bee will possibly make an error of one degree for each four minutes he spends on his way back to the hive.

Yet, the bee does not actually have any problem at all! The bee's eye is formed of many small hexagonal lenses. Each lens focuses on a narrow area just like a telescope. When the bee flies towards the sun during the day, it can find its exact position all the time. Scientists say that the bee does this by judging the time of day by the brightness of the sun. It accordingly modifies its directions to the other bees so that there is no margin of error.

HONEY MIRACLE

∾

Your Lord inspired the bee, saying: ...."eat of all the produce of the earth, and find with skill the spacious paths of your Lord: there issues from within their bodies a drink of varying colours, wherein is healing for men: surely in this there is a Sign for those who would give thought." (An-Nahl, 69)

It has become possible only in the last few years, with the improvements in research techniques, to analyze the content of the honey and its significance as a food source. Many international magazines have used honey as a cover page story, while others have even gone further and prepared additional issues for this precious natural food. Now let us look into the details of this unbelievable nutrient produced by this very small animal that Allah has created:

Honey is composed of sugars like glucose, fructose and minerals like magnesium, calcium, sodium, chlorine, sulfur, iron and phosphate. In addition to these, honey includes Vitamins B1, B2, C, B6, B5 and B3, their concentration differing according to the pollen and nectar sources. Copper, iodine, iron and zinc also exist in it in small quantities, plus, several kinds of hormones.

"During the World Apiculture Conference held on 20-26 September, 1993, in China, treatments with honey derivatives were discussed. American scientists stressed that honey, royal jelly, pollen and "propolis" (bee resin) had the capability of curing many illnesses. One Romanian doctor stated that he used honey for the treatment of patients with cataracts, and 2002 of his 2094 patients recovered completely. Polish doctors also gave information about bee resin's curative properties for diseases like hemorrhoids, skin problems, women's illnesses and many others. Nowadays, apiculture and bee products are the object of research in developed countries." (Hurriyet Newspaper, October 19, 1993)

Scientists agree upon the fact that even a spoonful of honey is absolutely beneficial to the body, because the sugar molecules in the honey can turn into other types of sugar (fructose to glucose) and despite its high acid concentration, it is easily digested even by the most sensitive stomachs. It also helps the kidneys to function better. Another interesting aspect of honey is that, when it is compared with the same amount of sugar, it gives 40% less calories to the body. This quality of the honey prevents weight-gain.

Rapidly fuses with the blood: Honey enters the circulatory system in 7 minutes when taken with tepid water and in 20 minutes when taken with cold water. The free sugar molecules in it make it easier for the brain to function.

Promotes production of blood: Honey functions as the energy store for new blood formation and helps anemic people by speeding up this process. It helps in the purification and nourishment of the blood. Blood circulation is regulated by it. It also has positive effects on capillary problems.

Friend of the stomach: Honey does not result in acidose or alcoholic fermentation because of its fast digestion. The free radicals within it make it easier for the fats to be digested. It makes up for the absence of iron in the milk of mothers and cows. While improving intestinal functions, it gives inner comfort, and increases the appetite.

Royal jelly: Royal jelly is the white fluid produced by worker bees inside the beehive. In this nutritious substance, there is sugar, protein, fat and many vitamins. It is used when the body is left weak and in problems that occur because of tissue aging.

Bacteria killing property: The bacteria-killing property of the honey is called the "inhibition effect". Experiments carried out on honey showed that its bacteria-killing effect doubled when diluted with water. It is very interesting to observe that the newborn bees are also fed with diluted honey by the nurse bees responsible for taking care of them.

THE CAMEL

ॐ

"Do not they look at the camel; how it is created?

This 17th verse of Al-Gashiya chapter tells us that the camel is an animal that has to be carefully examined. The first things that come to the mind when one thinks of the camel is hot weather, drought and deserts. The toughness of the desert conditions where the camel serves people, gives rise to questions which need clear answers. These are:
- Thirst
- Too high temperatures during day time
- Too low temperatures during night time
- Need for food
- Barrenness of the land
- Natural events like storms and whirlwinds
- Energy requirements, etc.

The camel is created in such a way as to resolve all of the above questions, making it eminently suitable to meet the needs of human comfort and convenience.

Now, let us take a quick glance at its abilities and characteristics:

Resistance to thirst and hunger: Camels can live without food or water for 8 days in 50-degree celcius temperatures.

Improved water utilization unit: In a mere 10 minutes, camels can consume 130 liters of water, which is around one third of their body weight. Camels also have a curvy mucus structure in their nose that has a 100 times larger area than the human's nose. With this structure, camels can have the benefit of about 66% of the moisture in the air.

Maximum benefit from food and water: Most animals die when the accumulated urea in their bodies mixes with the blood in the circulatory system. Yet, camels use this urea by passing it through the liver continuously in order to use it as a protein and water source. The hump is another aid to the camel. One fifth of the camel's body is stored in the form of fat in its hump. The storage of the body fat in only one part of the camel's body prevents it from using water all through its body. This allows its body to use the minimum amount of water.

Although a camel with humps can take in 30-50 kg of food in a day, it is able to live for one month on only 2 kg. of grass. Camels have very strong rubber-like lips, which permit them to eat thorns sharp enough to pierce leather. Moreover, they possess such a strong digestive system that they can eat everything in sight, like plastic plates, copper wire and reeds. The four-chambered stomach of this wonderful animal is designed to cater for non-food substances as well, which increases its chances of obtaining energy from sources other than food. This adaptability is definitely helpful in surviving in an arid region.

Protection against whirlwinds and storms: The eyes of camels have two rows of eyelashes. The structure of the eyelashes is like two different combs clamping together which protect the eyes from severe sandstorms. Another advantage of this design is the protection of the eyes from strong sunrays. Remarkably, camels can close the openings of their noses in these kinds of storms.

Protection against burning and freezing weather conditions: Thick hair on the camel's body prevents the burning sunlight from penetrating its skin. This helps the animal to keep cool which in turn increases water-retention and reduces dehydration by lessening the risk of sweating profusely. This thick hair on the skin also protects the animal against very cold weather. While desert camels are not affected by high temperatures up to 70 degrees Celsius, double-humped camels can survive in cold weather with temperatures going down to -52 degrees Celsius. This kind of camel can survive even in high mountains 4000 m. above sea level.

Protection from burning hot sand: The feet of the camel, being very large in proportion to its body, helps the animal not to get stuck in the sand because of its weight. The special thick skin on the soles of the camel's feet acts as a protection from not desert sand.

THE CAMEL AS A BEAST OF BURDEN

∾

"And they carry your heavy loads to lands that you could not otherwise reach except with souls distressed: for your Lord is indeed Most Kind, Most Merciful" (Nahl Sura, 7)

Camels are very strong animals. They can travel a distance of 40 kilometers with a load of 250 kilograms, and without any load, they can travel for 300 kilometers. Because of this capability, camels are called the "ships of the desert". Has the camel adapted its body to suit desert conditions? Has it formed its own nose mucus or the hump on its back?

The rhetorical question in the Qur'an: "Do they not look at the camel, how it is created?" Suggests the awe we should feel at this excellent example of Allah's creativity.

THE GNAT

❧

"Allah does not disdain to give a parable about a gnat,
or a larger creative."

As proof of His magnificence and power, Allah indiscriminately
provides examples of all animals, whether as massive as a camel
or as small as a bee, for they all serve extremely important
purposes. "Not without purpose did We create heaven and
earth and all between!" Even the whole universe is given as
an example for human beings to learn from.

> *"Allah does not disdain to give a parable about gnat,*
> *or a larger creature. Those who believe know that¹ it*
> *is truth from their Lord; but those who reject Faith*
> *say: 'What does Allah mean by this parable?' By it*
> *He causes many to stray, and many He leads to the*
> *right path; but He causes none to stray, except those*
> *who forsake the right path"* (Al-Baqara, 26)

Contrary to common belief, gnats, which we frequently
encounter, are indeed very complex creatures.

Gnats see the creatures around them in different colours
according to their body temperatures. Because their sensing of
the temperature is not dependent on daylight, they see the

warm-blooded capillaries as dark-red even in a dark room. This is why gnats never have any problem in finding a food source. These sensitive sensory receptors of the gnat can easily identify a change in the temperature , even by a fraction of a degree.

Here we have mentioned only a few examples. Yet, the perfect creation of Allah can easily be observed in nature. The real purpose of nature's existence is a tangible proof of the perfect creation and intelligence of Allah. The only way to realize this is to make a sincere evaluation of everything with a "seeing" eye and a "thinking" mind. Thus, the detailed and marvellous order existing in the universe will be observed much better.

> "He created the seven heavens one above another: no want of proportion will you see in the Creation of Allah the Most Merciful. Then look once more and yet again: your eyes will in the end grow dim and weary." Again turn thy vision a second time: (thy) vision will come back to thee dull and discomfited, in a state worn out." (Al-Mulk, 3-4)

> "Do they not travel through the land, so that their hearts and minds may thus learn wisdom and their ears may thus learn to hear? Truly, it is not their eyes that are blind, but their hearts which are in their breasts." (Al-Hajj 46)

> "Do you not see that Allah has subjected to your use all things in the heavens and on earth, and lavished upon you his favours, both seen and unseen? Yet there are among men those who dispute about Allah, without knowledge and without guidance, and without a Book to enlighten them! " (Luqman, 20)

> "Say: 'Travel through the earth and see how Allah originated creation; so then Allah will produce a later creation: for Allah has power over all things.'" (Al-Ankaboot, 20)

"Not without purpose did We create heaven and earth and all between! That is the fancy of the unbelievers! But woe to the unbelievers when they are cast into the Fire of Hell!" (Sad, 27)

"He has subjected to you, as from Him, all that is in the heavens and on earth: Surely, these are Signs in this for those who reflect." (Al-Jathiya, 13)

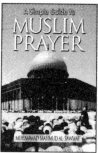

ISBN 81-87570-26-1

ISBN 81-87570-71-7

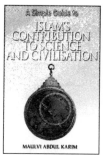

ISBN 81-87570-45-8

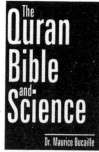

ISBN 81-87570-53-9

ISBN 81-87570-67-9

ISBN 81-87570-52-0

ISBN 81-87570-61-X

ISBN 81-87570-16-4

ISBN 81-87570-90-7

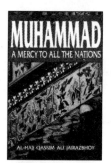

ISBN 81-87570-14-8

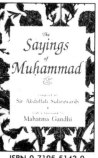

ISBN 0-7195-5143-9

ISBN 81-85063-38-9

ISBN 81-85063-68-0

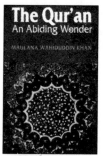

ISBN 81-85063-73-7

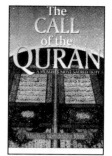

ISBN 81-87570-03-2

ISBN 81-85063-84-2

Man Know Thyself

Maulana Wahiduddin Khan

Search for Truth

Maulana Wahiduddin Khan

The Concept of God

Maulana Wahiduddin Khan

The Creation Plan of God

Maulana Wahiduddin Khan

The Man Islam Builds

Maulana Wahiduddin Khan

Non-Violence and Islam

Maulana Wahiduddin Khan

Islamic Fundamentalism

Maulana Wahiduddin Khan

The Shariah and Its Application

Maulana Wahiduddin Khan

Muhammad: The Ideal Character

Maulana Wahiduddin Khan

Polygamy and Islam

Maulana Wahiduddin Khan

Uniform Civil Code
A CRITICAL STUDY

Maulana Wahiduddin Khan

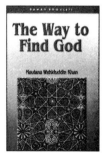

The Way to Find God

Maulana Wahiduddin Khan

The Teachings of Islam

Maulana Wahiduddin Khan

The Good Life

Maulana Wahiduddin Khan

The Garden of Paradise

Maulana Wahiduddin Khan

The Fire of Hell

Maulana Wahiduddin Khan

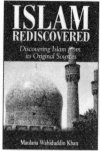

ISBN 81-87570-40-7

ISBN 81-87570-69-5

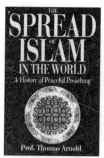

ISBN 81-87570-22-9

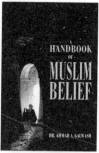

ISBN 81-87570-46-6

ISBN 81-87570-20-2

ISBN 81-87570-55-5

ISBN 81-87570-56-3

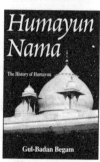

ISBN 81-87570-99-7

ISBN 81-87570-62-8

ISBN 81-87570-18-0

ISBN 81-87570-63-6

ISBN 81-87570-68-7

ISBN 81-85063-29-X

ISBN 81-85063-34-6

ISBN 81-85063-27-3

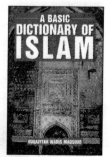

ISBN 81-85063-30-3